t date

D1587357

800 752 733

KIRKLEES LIBRARIES

Deliciously Balanced Asian Meals in 30 Minutes or Less

WOK ON

Ching-He Huang

For my mum and dad, my No.1 fans.

Ching-He Huang is an Emmy-nominated TV chef and cookery author. Born in Taipei, Taiwan, her culinary ethos is to use fresh, organic, ethically sourced ingredients to create modern dishes that fuse Chinese tradition with innovation and are accessible for home cooks. Her immensely popular TV series include *Chinese Food Made Easy*, *Chinese Food in Minutes*, *Exploring China* and *Ching's Amazing Asia*. She has also been a regular guest chef on *Saturday Kitchen* and *This Morning*.

Ching has written eight bestselling cookbooks: *Stir Crazy*, *Eat Clean: Wok Yourself to Health*, *Exploring China*, *Ching's Fast Food*, *Everyday Easy Chinese*, *Ching's Chinese Food in Minutes*, *Chinese Food Made Easy* and *China Modern*. She is also the creator of The Lotus Wok – a wok with a dynamic nano-silica coating for high performance cooking. Ching divides her time between the UK, the US and Asia.

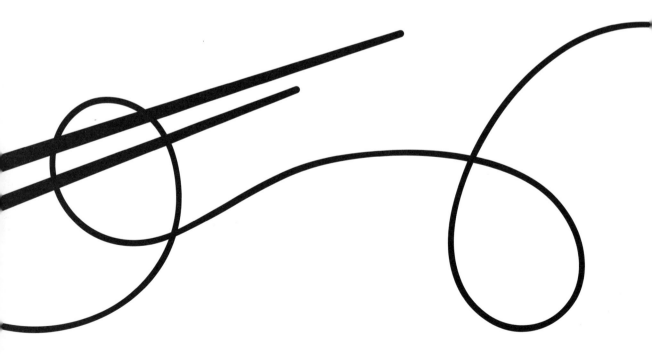

Deliciously Balanced Asian Meals in 30 Minutes or Less

WOK ON

Ching-He Huang

Kyle Books

An Hachette UK Company
www.hachette.co.uk

First published in Great Britain in 2019 by
Kyle Books, an imprint of Kyle Cathie Ltd
Carmelite House
50 Victoria Embankment
London EC4Y 0DZ
www.kylebooks.co.uk

ISBN: 978 0 85783 633 5

Text copyright 2019 © Ching-He Huang
Design and layout copyright 2019 © Kyle Cathie Ltd

Ching-He Huang is hereby identified as the author
of this work in accordance with section 77 of the
Copyright, Designs and Patents Act 1988.

All rights reserved. No part of this work may be
reproduced or utilised in any form or by any means,
electronic or mechanical, including photocopying,
recording or by any information storage and retrieval
system, without the prior written permission of the
publisher.

Publisher: Joanna Copestick
Editorial Director: Judith Hannam
Editorial Assistant: Isabel Gonzalez-Prendergast
Design: Caroline Clark
Photography: Tamin Jones
Food styling: Aya Nishimura
Props styling: Wei Tang
Production: Gemma John

A Cataloguing in Publication record for this title is
available from the British Library.

Printed and bound in China

10 9 8 7 6 5 4 3 2 1

INTRODUCTION

Ni hao! Hello!

Thank you so much for picking up *Wok On!* I very much hope it will inspire you to take up a wok and get cooking. I know it's not always easy to stay motivated and make meals from scratch, but I've been doing this a while and, I promise you, home-wokked dishes using fresh ingredients are always going to be better for your health and deliver more in terms of live enzymes and micro-nutrients than ready meals. The trick is to make it fun, and soon you'll be on your wokstar journey – I apologise now in advance for the wok jokes! There'll be plenty! #Wokscooking!

Wok On follows on from my *Stir Crazy* cookbook, which was all about stir fries. *Wok On* also includes stir-fried dishes, but also focuses on the techniques you may not have considered when using your wok – braising, steaming, shallow frying and deep frying. My aim is to show you that armed with this one-pan wonder you can make a huge variety of meals for you and your family.

I have included new, occasionally crazy (though in a good way!) recipes such as My Sriracha Ketchup Prawns, Kirakuya Fireballs, Dirty Hoisin Cranberry Kimchi Pork and Hot Cheese Sandwich, Golden Sesame Prawn Balls, Hoisin Duck and Strawberry Wok-Fried Crispy Wonton 'Tacos' and Macanese-style Codfish and Potato Balls, which might raise a few eyebrows, but I promise they are all utterly delicious.

If you are after ease and speed, I have plenty of delicious options, including some re-worked takeaway favourites. Designed with busy wokkers like you in mind, they are simple enough for everyday cooking and super healthy too. They include dishes such as Prawn 'Ban' Mein, Wok-Fried Beef in Chilli Sauce with Coriander, Spicy Smoked Bacon Broccoli, and failproof Crabmeat Sweetcorn Soup, as well as Chinese-in-taste comfort foods such as Taiwanese-style Seafood 'Pancake', Ching's Fish Ball Noodle Soup, Drunken Scallops with Samphire, Soy Beansprout Coriander Cheung Fun Rolls, Chicken with Ginger Choi Sum and Goji Berries and Sichuan Bacon and Leek Wok-Fry.

And since there is a growing demand for vegan food (my husband is vegan), I have included many recipes that are vegan. In fact, Chinese vegetarian food is mostly vegan (if you omit eggs) as we use virtually no dairy in our cuisine and instead rely on tofu, mushrooms and other vegetables and nuts. So if you are looking to eat more vegetables, most of the meat dishes can be made vegan with a few simple substitutes. Some of my favourites are Sichuan Chilli Tomato Mock Chicken, Saucy Mushroom and Ginger Tofu, Sichuan Spicy Salt and Pepper Mock Duck, Veggie 'Pork' Mince with French Beans, Vietnamese-Style Golden Tofu Noodle Salad, Vegan Pho and Thai Green Sweet Potato Curry.

If you love to entertain and are looking for variety and versatile dishes, then this book is for you. I love to entertain and often double up the recipes for a Chinese-style buffet for family and friends. You can have something in the steamer, on the pot, in the oven or rice cooker and then a couple of woks on the go! My Macanese Minchi is great for a Sunday brunch, Mock Duck Black Pepper with Basil Shen Jian Bao are great as party food, Oxtail and Turnip Noodle Soup is easy to do for a large crowd for dinner, Golden Macanese Cod, Crispy 'Family Snapper' with Black Bean Sauce, Miso Honey Ribs, Vegan Crispy 'Bottom' 'Guoh Teh' Vegetable Dumplings, Moreish Crispy Seaweed, Ching's Braised Hong Sao Pork, Beef and Mushroom Beijing-style Wheat Flour Pancakes, Beef and Pea Wontons and Pearly Beef Balls are great family friendly dim sum dishes. My dumpling and dim sum recipes can also be frozen so all you need to do is boil, steam or wok-fry when you need them.

And if, like me, you're a fan of rice dishes, I have plenty to satisfy your taste-buds, from Black Pepper Bacon Pineapple Fried Rice, Smoked Salmon and Egg Fried Rice to Japanese Rice Omelette (Omu-Raisu) to Pork, Kimchi and Water Chestnut Fried Rice and Black Pepper Duck and Kale Wokked Rice; there is something for everyone.

I've also discovered a love of fusing dishes and in particular draw quite a bit of inspiration from Macao, a small region just off the South China Sea, fusing Portuguese, African, Indian and Chinese influences. In terms of re-discovery,

perhaps my favourite 'seasoning' or flavour pairing in *Wok On* is oyster sauce (mushroom sauce if you are vegan) and black pepper – the result is an addictive and powerful flavour combination! A little of the seasoning goes a long way. I don't like to over-season my food and am always careful not to go overboard on the sodium, preferring to use low-sodium light soy sauce where possible. Which brings me to ingredients. I choose organic and higher welfare whenever possible – it's much better for both you and the planet.

So, this book is designed for you to make it your own – to make substitutions and add vegetables you prefer. Whether it's a saucy dish, or a dry noodle fry that you are after, whether you're a meat or veggie vegan lover, a novice or a total wokstar, I hope the dishes will help you increase your kitchen repertoire and bring some balance to your eating.

So enough chatting, let's get wokking!

Wok on my friends and I sincerely wish you happy eating always!

Love,

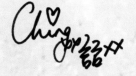

WHY USE A WOK?

Why use a wok?

The ultimate kitchen implement, this 2,000-year-old magical cooking pot is a way of life all over Asia. Perfect for sautéing, braising, frying and steaming, it can be a lifesaver on busy days.

How do I go about choosing a wok?

My grandmother used to cook in a cast-iron wok, and they are the best, but they are extremely heavy, and it can be difficult to toss the food or manoeuvre them away from the hob when the heat gets too hot.

Most Chinese chefs use unseasoned carbon steel woks, but these require a lot of love and care or they rust. Non-stick varieties are available but are not ideal as the coating comes off with time. Some carbon steel woks have a flat, wide base more like a saucepan, which is not a traditional wok shape, so look for ones with deep sides (to allow you to toss the food) and a small centre (to concentrate the heat). Traditional woks are round-bottomed, but these require a wok ring set over your hob, which is another added piece of equipment and not ideal for the modern home, especially induction hobs.

Stainless-steel woks need to be seasoned with coatings of apple cider vinegar, each coating evaporated to give a clear, thin non-stick layer. They are particularly good if you are into healthy eating, but don't retain heat as well as carbon steel and sometimes have uneven heat spots, which means food can stick.

Aluminium woks are inexpensive, but they can rust and warp and are not as good at either conducting or retaining heat as carbon steel woks.

Whatever wok you have, I always say it's best to use it and not waste it. When it's on its last legs and you need a replacement, please do seek out my Lotus Wok. I designed it for people who want a better wok experience. It is inexpensive and is made from carbon steel so that it heats quickly, plus it has a natural, 'non-stick'-type, nano-silica coating (made from sand-blasted crystals). It is a medium gauge, so not too heavy yet not flimsy. It's also scratch-resistant, so you can use metal utensils on it, and hydrophobic, which means it repels water, giving your veggies that crisp finish, and oleophilic, which means it allows just enough oil to coat the surface of the wok. It is a clever wok that just gets better with time – I have used mine for over three years now and it is still going strong. It comes with a wooden spatula, a glass lid and a stainless-steel steamer rack. You can purchase it on amazon.co.uk, or for more information, check out www.chinghehuang.com.

Now you have a wok, what's the first step?

If you don't need to season your new wok, you can go right ahead and start cooking – just use a damp sponge and a little soapy water to wash off any industrial oil, dust or dirt, rinse, then place it on the heat to dry. If you need to season your wok, go to my online video at www.youtube.com/user/chinghehuang, which shows you how.

The 'Breath of the Wok'

Home wok cooking differs from restaurant wok cooking as the latter has wok burners that can reach 650°C (far higher than the 180°C that the average domestic hob can achieve), but the one thing that differentiates a good stir-fry from a bad one is the 'breath of the wok', a term used to describe the wok-hei – the 'smoky flavour' that comes from a good flame-wokked dish, and the all-important balance of *xiang, se, wei* (the aroma, colour and taste of the overall dish). Wok chefs in restaurants manoeuvre and operate a gas lever by the side of their legs at the same time as they toss the wok and flick it towards the flames so they lick the sides of the wok, injecting wok smoke into the dish. This is why I have so much respect for wok chefs – they have no fear of the flames, which can sometimes be over 2 metres high. They inject the 'breath of the wok' into the dish, as well as sauté, sear, deep-fry, shallow-fry, steam and braise, all in one cooking vessel, or have the eye-to-hand-to-leg body co-ordination (wok dance as I often refer to it) to time the addition of each ingredient perfectly. Cooking on such high heat means that if you are one second out your vegetables lose their shine or crispness, and is why perfect stir-frying is so hard to master. Consistent results take practice, timing, skill and unwavering focus. However, this doesn't mean that you can't still get those smoky delicious results from wokking at home! I have some tips to help you.

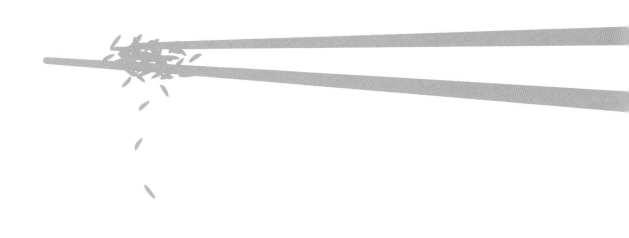

WOKKING TECHNIQUES

STIR FRYING

This is perhaps the most classic use for a wok – a little bit of oil and lots of stirring will ensure that ingredients keep their crunch and take on a delicious smoky flavour. For stir frying, there are ways to help you get it as perfect as possible.

Preparation is key!

Ensure all your ingredients are prepped beforehand and are as close to the wok as possible to save you time, and arm yourself with the freshest ingredients. If ingredients are substandard, you will be able to tell, because vegetables will not look fresh or bright and, once stir-fried, they will go limp very quickly. When it's 'wok on', there is no time to do anything – least of all, to stop and chop!

The right oils

An odourless, flavourless oil that has a high smoke point, such as peanut oil, rapeseed oil or coconut oil, is best – it gives a neutral base on which to create your layers of flavour, yet is able to withstand high temperatures. Toasted sesame oil is really only used for seasoning.

What level of heat should I go for?

It's important to get your wok really hot before adding anything, so that you see a little smoke rising off the surface. At that point, it's time to quickly add the oil, which will heat up instantly. Heating the wok first means the heat is evenly distributed over the entire surface. Once you add ingredients to it, the temperature in the wok starts to fall, but keep the ingredients moving to prevent them burning or take the wok away from the heat source. If you are really worried about the flame, then heat the wok over a medium-high heat and work your way up to maximum heat over the course of several stir-fries where practice becomes perfect.

Size and shape matters

Whenever you add several ingredients to the wok at the same time – for example, aromatics such as garlic, ginger, chillies and small pieces of onion, or different types of vegetables, such as shredded cabbage, carrot and onions – it's important they are all a similar size as this will ensure they cook in the same amount of time.

It's important, too, to consider the size of the main protein ingredient in relation to the rest of the ingredients. For example, if you are wokking beef slices, then make sure the vegetables are cut in slices too, so that the dish looks balanced. How you cut the ingredients is very important. If you slice on a deep diagonal, it exposes more surface area for cooking and it can also make ingredients go that much further. For example, wafer-thin, square-ish slices can be achieved by slicing across the grain of a cut of beef. Vegetables can be prepared in the same way, so a carrot can be sliced into round coins or into long oval pieces if sliced on the diagonal. Play with the shape and have fun!

Balance the aromatics – the awesome foursome!

I like to use a combination of garlic, ginger and chillies – what I call The Holy Trinity – but now

I sometimes add spring onions to the mix too. Holy Trinity was so last year – now it's all about the Awesome Foursome! I have been accused of adding garlic, ginger and chillies in almost all my dishes, but this is because I try to inject their healthful, anti-bacterial properties into my cooking as much as possible, so that I am getting the maximum healthful nutrients in any one meal. But it is entirely up to you and you can vary what you add to suit your likes and mood, of course.

'Compartment' cooking

Compartmentalise your ingredients – group aromatics together, also the vegetables, and seasonings. Think of your protein and treat it separately – what flavours are you trying to achieve? Finally, think of your garnishes and ways to inject some freshness into the dish at the end. So, break the recipe down. Sometimes the dish looks like a long list of ingredients but actually most are store cupboard ingredients, and garnishes. So, the dishes are not as long or as difficult as they may first 'appear' – after all – appearances are deceptive!

STEAMING

Food cooked in this way is super healthy! You can use a bamboo steamer and set this on a wok, or now stainless-steel or bamboo racks can be set on top of a wok and all you have to do is pop the lid on. Both are relatively inexpensive. Bamboo steamers are versatile in that you can pile a few compartments on top of each other so you can steam multiple dishes at once, and whilst steaming they also give off a light bamboo fragrance. The stainless-steel rack is good as it lasts a lot longer. Here are a few things to note before you wok steam!

Make sure the wok is stable

If you have a flat-bottomed wok, this will be fine, but if you have a round-bottomed one, then invest in a wok stand as well as you don't want to risk spilling over hot water and steam. Safety first!

How much water do I fill the wok with?

Fill the wok half full with boiling water and place the bamboo steamer on the top, making sure the base of the steamer does not touch the water. Depending on the recipe, either place the food to be steamed on a heatproof plate, bowl or shallow bowl that fits in the steamer, or on greaseproof paper, or on bits of food (for example, dumplings can be set on top of a small slice of carrot for function and presentation purposes). Put the lid on and steam. If necessary, top up the wok with more boiling water as the food cooks. The trick is to make sure the bamboo steamer or rack you are using is stable, fits comfortably and securely within the wok and that there is minimal room for steam to escape, so the size of the steamer and how it fits across the wok is important, and the key is to find one that is big enough to steam a large amount and fits snugly across the wok. You can pile up to three bamboo steamers high, any more and you may need a more powerful burner to create enough steam to reach the highest part of the steamer.

Hot steam

Before you attempt to take off the lid of the steamer, just take care and make sure you turn the hob off first. Gently lift the lid away from you, so the hot steam wafts away from you and you don't burn your arms.

DEEP FRYING

Deep frying gets a bad rap as it's deemed an unhealthy way of cooking. Now, of course, it isn't as healthy as a virtuous steamed dish, and it's much more sinful than a stir fry, however, deep frying as a technique is not as bad as you might think. If the food is dropped into hot enough oil, the outside edges are sealed at a high temperature and so the heat will continue to cook the food, and not allow any further oil to be absorbed into the food.

So the most important tip (apart from having a stable and secure wok – please refer to my wok stand tip in the steaming section), is to make sure the oil is at the correct temperature. For best results, invest in a good deep-frying thermometer and follow the recommended temperatures in my recipes. If the oil is not hot enough, the food will take longer to cook and the result is greasy food. If the temperature is too high, the food will burn on the outside while the inside doesn't cook through. If you don't have a thermometer then I would use the bread or ginger test – add a cube or a small or piece of bread or ginger to the hot oil, and if it turns golden brown in 15 seconds, the oil is at 180°C, or thereabouts.

When you are ready to fry, use a slotted spoon or a Chinese 'spider' – like a web-like mesh scooper; both also work well as a strainer. Use it to lift fried foods out – it helps to drain as much oil in the process – then place the food onto a plate lined with kitchen paper.

The 'spiders' are available in Chinese supermarkets and they come in various sizes; the handles are often made from bamboo.

When you start deep-frying, make sure the wok is stable, do not overfill the wok with oil (it should never be more than half full as there is less chance of bubbling and food spilling over), make sure the food you are frying is not wet as it will spit in the hot oil, don't re-use oil if you can – it will give fresher results. Use a large pair of tongs or long wooden bamboo chopsticks to help turn the food if necessary, and don't use plastic utensils as they will melt.

Lastly, serve the dish immediately, as it will quickly start to lose its crunch and crispness. However, if avoidable, keep the food hot in a pre-heated oven before serving.

BRAISING

There are a few recipes that require a quick 20-minute braise. You can wok fry and brown the meats and then add some stock and the seasonings for a quick saucy or brothy dish. The results are fabulous in a wok because the deep sides can allow you to add as much liquid as you want and at the end of the cooking process if you want to add vegetables or noodles, the wok has enough room to allow you to do that, for an easy one-pot dish. The same rules apply as with all wokking or cooking, make sure the wok is stable on the hob.

BOILING

The wok with its deep sides is great for boiling – especially for soup broths – and works just like a pot, allowing a lot of food and liquid to be contained in the wok – so you can boil to your heart's content!

SMOKING

Smoking is not a technique I use in any of the recipes in *Wok On* but it can be useful to smoke a small piece of fish or duck. The trick is to set the wok on hot, add fruit wood chips, Jasmine rice or whatever flavour you like, and place the stainless steel rack on top. Then place the meat, fish or tofu on a heatproof plate on top of the rack, close the lid, turn the heat to very low and let the smoking ingredients at the base gently burn to create smoke for your dish.

EQUIPMENT

In my recipes, I like to keep equipment to a minimum – apart from a good, flat-bottomed wok and wok lid, all you need is an all-purpose chef's knife (or I like to use a Chinese cleaver), a chopping board and a wooden spatula for stir frying. Best to keep things simple. It's not about fancy equipment, rather more robust, functional equipment that you will use time and again.

COOK'S NOTES

Salt the oil
Some Chinese chefs swear that seasoning the oil with a pinch of salt before adding the aromatics helps to retain the colour of the vegetables. It means the salt flavour is evenly distributed throughout, and you don't get any large, undissolved flakes of salt in the finished dish.

Meats
If you are on a budget, you can use less expensive cuts. These are usually tougher, but the trick is to use a couple of very small pinches of bicarbonate of soda to tenderise the meat. My philosophy is to use free-range or organic where possible; yes, it is expensive, but I prefer quality over quantity. It is up to you whether you go for the cheaper or expensive meat option, just always make sure you season the meat first with a pinch of salt, ground white pepper and a dusting of cornflour to help the meat taste that much juicier. You can also add a pinch of Chinese five-spice, turmeric, dried chillies, fennel seeds or ground coriander to inject flavour into the meat.

Water is your best friend
When the wok gets too hot to handle, water is your best friend. Having a small jug of cold water to hand and knowing when to add a drop is important, especially if your ingredients are beginning to burn. If you are making a one-wok dish where you 'don't return' (in Mandarin, *hui guo*) any ingredient to the wok, you will need to deglaze it after cooking individual ingredients and you will need some liquid in between these additions to help each group of ingredients cook. Generally, this is after the protein and again once the vegetables have gone in. When stir-frying tender leaf vegetables, after the oil and aromatics have gone in, adding a small amount of water around the edge of the wok will help to steam-cook the vegetables, ready for seasoning.

Quick homemade sauces and seasonings
From sriracha and oyster to garlic hoisin, you can create sweet, sour and spicy sauces that will complement your dishes, whether you use them as cook-in sauces or dressings on the side. Think of your condiment cupboard like a bar, where you are the mixologist, creating your own sauces.

Soybean pastes
I can't live without soybean pastes – the flavour combinations are limitless, with endless umami possibilities. My favourites include fermented salted dried black beans (soybeans dried and salted in the sun – just give them a rinse in water, then crush and mix into Shaohsing rice wine to make a paste), Japanese salty miso paste (which comes in red and white varieties – great for soups, stir-fries, sauces, dressings and marinades), and the Korean chilli paste gochujang.

Curry/Spice pastes
I love to experiment with South East Asian curry pastes such as Thai red curry, Thai green curry, yellow curry, and so on, and not just to make curry, but for stir-frying and in noodle soups. I also love chilli pastes and sambals from Malaysia,

as well as spice mixes and tamarind paste, which give a sour kick and an exotic South East Asian taste to my dishes.

Cornflour/Potato flour

This is an all-important store cupboard ingredient because it helps to bind the flavours in the wok to the protein and vegetables. Traditionally, a technique called 'velveting' was the norm when cooking meat. It involved coating strips of meat with egg white and cornflour to give it a silky texture when shallow-fried. However, I've designed a new way to enhance the flavour of the meat without the shallow-frying step – I season the meat first with salt and ground white pepper, then dust with cornflour or potato flour. This helps to seal in the juices as the meat hits the oil. The trick to making sure it doesn't stick to the wok is to let it brown for 10 seconds before flipping it to cook on the other side. Don't worry if the meat catches – those slightly burnt edges all add to the flavour. You can also loosen the flavours in the wok by using a small drop of water or Shaohsing rice wine to deglaze the pan.

In some of the dishes, the cornflour is also mixed with cold water to create a blended paste that is usually added at the end of the cooking to thicken the sauce and give it a shine. In others, where I group ingredients together for a more complex flavour, I like to add the cornflour to the ingredients for the sauce – just ensure that the liquid, whether water or stock, is cold, so that the sauce doesn't thicken before it's added to the wok (you want the sauce to thicken and caramelise in the wok, not in the jug).

Dofu/Tofu

Dofu (which is the Mandarin name) or tofu (Japanese) is an excellent source of protein, iron, calcium, manganese, selenium, phosphorus, copper, magnesium, vitamin B1 and zinc. It also contains all nine essential amino acids. Available fresh, fried, smoked, firm and silken, it's a great protein alternative for vegans and vegetarians – it features heavily in Buddhist Chinese cuisine. Try to get organic tofu or that made from sprouted soy though – and stay away from GM soy.

Spices

To get the best out of your spices, particularly whole ones such as Sichuan peppercorns, first dry toast them in a wok or small pan and then grind them in a pestle and mortar or clean coffee grinder.

Aromatics

Whether you do so with spring onions, fresh coriander, mint, raw beansprouts, nuts or seeds, Japanese nori seaweed, chilli flakes or a wedge of lemon or lime, adding a fragrant aromatic garnish to your stir-fry at the end will enhance your dish, so give it a go and experiment.

Rice and nutritious grains

For most of my dishes, unless it's a chow mein, jasmine rice is my rice of choice. You can also use other grains and pulses mixed into it, which is something I do when trying to eat more healthily. For example, I sometimes mix jasmine rice, wild rice and green lentils. Basmati is a good option for fried rice, as it is more robust. Brown rice is high in fibre as well as being delicious, and can be mixed with jasmine rice, wild rice and chickpeas to create a different bite.

Noodles

It's best to pre-cook noodles according to the packet instructions, then drain and drizzle some toasted sesame oil over to prevent them from sticking together. For low-carb and wheat-free options, try mung bean noodles, soybean noodles, sweet potato noodles, shirataki and rice noodles. I also love the traditional wheat flour noodles, which come in several varieties, such as buckwheat, somen, ramen, udon and egg.

Eggs

All eggs used in these recipes are medium unless otherwise specified. Whenever possible, use organic or free-range chicken and eggs as they will taste so much better.

Gluten-Free

Many dishes can be gluten-free if you omit wheat gluten/wheatflour noodles and use tamari instead of low-sodium light soy sauce. There are many gluten-free substitutes available at specialist producers online.

VEGAN &

VEGETARIAN

VIETNAMESE-STYLE GOLDEN TOFU NOODLE SALAD

3 x 50g blocks dried mung bean thread noodles

1 tablespoon rapeseed oil

500ml groundnut or sunflower oil

100g fresh firm tofu, drained and sliced into 1cm strips

70g toasted cashew nuts

80g blanched beansprouts

handful of mint leaves

1 small red chilli, deseeded and finely chopped lengthways

For the dressing

4 tablespoons mirin

2–3 tablespoons runny honey

2 tablespoons grated lemongrass

2 tablespoons tamari or low-sodium light soy sauce

4 mint leaves, shredded

4 tablespoons lime juice

2 small red chillies, deseeded and chopped

This is a delicious and easy vegan noodle salad. If you are not vegan, you can use fish sauce instead of tamari; it will give a richness to the flavour. The slippery texture of mung bean noodles (also known as vermicelli glass noodles because of their translucent look) is great in this dish. Not only are they low in calories, they are also an absolute joy to eat! If you can't get hold of them, use vermicelli rice noodles, and if you don't eat honey, you can use golden syrup. Bon appetit!

Serves 4 kcal 390 carbs 55g protein 7.4g fat 15.9g

Cook the mung bean noodles in a pan of boiling water for 3 minutes, then drain and rinse under cold running water and cut the noodles into approx. 5mm pieces so they are easier to eat and don't clump together. Place in a large bowl, cover with clingfilm and refrigerate. Drizzle over the rapeseed oil to prevent the noodles from sticking together.

Combine all the dressing ingredients in a bowl, blend well and set aside.

Heat a wok over a high heat, fill to a third of its depth with groundnut or sunflower oil. Heat the oil to 180°C or until a bread cube dropped in the oil turns golden brown in 15 seconds and floats to the surface. Add the tofu strips and fry for 8 minutes, until golden brown at the edges. Drain on a plate lined with kitchen paper.

Just before serving, toss the toasted cashew nuts, blanched beansprouts, some of the mint leaves and the chopped chilli into the noodles. Pour some of the dressing over the noodles and toss all together. Transfer to bowls, then place the fried tofu on top, drizzle with more dressing and garnish with more mint. Serve immediately.

15 mins

6 mins

Oven time: 30–35 mins

Ve GF DF

THAI GREEN SWEET POTATO CURRY

300g sweet potatoes, cut into
    2.5cm chunks
pinch of salt
1–2 tablespoons rapeseed oil

For the curry
1 tablespoon rapeseed oil
2.5cm piece of fresh ginger,
    peeled and grated
2 small baby shallots, sliced, or
    ½ white onion, diced
1 stalk of lemongrass, any tough
    outer leaf discarded, cut into
    4cm slices
2 tablespoons Thai green curry
    paste
1 tablespoon tamari or low-
    sodium light soy sauce
200ml coconut milk
300ml vegetable stock
pinch of salt
100g sugarsnap peas or
    mangetout, whole
Thai basil leaves
1 red chilli, seeds in, sliced

This dish is great on a cold winter's day. First, roast the sweet potatoes and then make a quick Thai green curry in the wok and serve with jasmine rice. Perfect in every way and so wholesome, yet easy to make, and above all – vegan too!

Serves 2 kcal 471 carbs 46.7g protein 5.1g fat 29.6g

Preheat the oven to 180°C, Gas Mark 4. Put the sweet potatoes on a baking tray and season with the salt and oil. Roast in the oven for 30–35 minutes.

For the curry, heat a wok over a medium heat, add the rapeseed oil and give the oil a swirl. Stir-fry the ginger, shallots or onion and lemongrass for a few seconds to release their aroma.

Add the Thai green curry paste and tamari or light soy sauce and stir around to distribute in the wok. Add the roasted sweet potatoes, followed by the coconut milk and vegetable stock and bring to the boil. The sweet potatoes should look lightly crisp and browned at the edges.

Add the salt and sugarsnap peas or mangetout and cook for 30 seconds. Garnish with the basil and sliced chilli. Spoon out and serve with jasmine rice.

20 mins

5–6 mins

Ve DF

MOCK FISH CAKES WITH CRISP CHINESE VEGETABLES

1 tablespoon rapeseed oil
2 garlic cloves, finely chopped
2.5cm piece of fresh ginger, peeled and grated
50g carrots, cut into julienne strips
50g baby corn, halved
50g water chestnuts, drained
80g broccoli, trimmed and cut into florets
80g mangetout
80g vegetarian mock fish cakes, halved
80g beansprouts
3 spring onions, sliced on an angle into 2.5cm pieces
2 tablespoons toasted sesame oil

For the sauce
2 tablespoons tamari or low-sodium light soy sauce
2 tablespoons vegetarian oyster sauce
2 tablespoons cornflour
2 tablespoons clear rice vinegar
200ml cold vegetable stock

A simple and delicious stir-fry full of veggie goodness that, served with rice, makes a quick and healthy mid-week supper.

Serves 2 kcal 372 carbs 40.4g protein 12.4g fat 21.2g

Combine all the ingredients for the sauce in a small jug, stir well and set aside.

Heat a wok over a high heat until the wok starts to smoke, then add the rapeseed oil and give the oil a swirl. Add the garlic and ginger and stir-fry for 10 seconds. Add all the remaining vegetables from the carrots to the mangetout and stir-fry for a further 2 minutes.

Stir the sauce mixture into the vegetables, then add the mock fish cakes and stir-fry for a further minute or so, until the liquid has thickened and the vegetables are glazed but still crisp. Stir in the beansprouts and spring onions and stir-fry for another 20 seconds. Season with the sesame oil and serve immediately with jasmine rice.

RED-COOKED TOFU WITH WHEAT FLOUR NOODLES

350g fried tofu, sliced into 1.5cm
     chunks
pinch of salt
pinch of ground white pepper
1 tablespoon cornflour or potato
     flour
1 tablespoon groundnut oil
2.5cm piece of fresh ginger,
     peeled and sliced
1 tablespoon five-spice mix
     (whole spices) including dried
     tangerine peel and cinnamon
     bark
1 tablespoon Shaohsing rice wine
     or dry sherry
150g dried wheat flour noodles,
     cooked according to packet
     instructions, drained, drizzled
     with toasted sesame oil
2 spring onions, finely sliced, to
     garnish

For the sauce
100ml cold vegetable stock
50ml light soy sauce
1 tablespoon dark soy sauce
1 tablespoon soft brown sugar
1 tablespoon cornflour

This famous cooking technique is unique to eastern China and is used primarily for stews and braised dishes. My grandmother used to cook in this way with belly pork and also added boiled eggs.

It's not the dish itself that is red, but the liquid. It makes a simple and delicious supper and is quick to cook, so I'm surprised it hasn't made its way onto takeaway menus.

Serves 4 kcal 454 carbs 44g protein 26.2g fat 19.7g

Combine all the ingredients for the sauce in a bowl, mix well and set aside.

Add the tofu to a bowl and season with the salt and white pepper, then add the cornflour or potato flour and mix well.

Heat a wok over a high heat until smoking, add the groundnut oil and give the oil a swirl. Add the ginger and the five-spice mix and stir-fry for a few seconds until fragrant, then add the tofu pieces and stir-fry for 2 minutes. Add the rice wine or dry sherry and cook for another 2 minutes, then add the sauce.

Once the sauce has reduced and is slightly sticky and a thicker consistency, take the wok off the heat.

Arrange the cooked noodles on serving plates and top with the tofu mixture. Garnish with the spring onions and serve immediately.

20 mins

2 mins

V DF

SOY MUSHROOM CRISPY CHINESE EGGS

2 tablespoons rapeseed oil

2 dried Chinese mushrooms, soaked in hot water for 20 minutes, drained, stalks discarded, sliced

1 teaspoon tamari or low-sodium light soy sauce

pinch of soft brown sugar

2 eggs

1 tablespoon chopped chives

To serve

1 tablespoon vegetarian oyster sauce mixed with 1 teaspoon sriracha chilli sauce

This makes the perfect umami breakfast dish. I love meaty Chinese mushrooms – in fact, I always keep a glass jar of soaking mushrooms in the fridge for when I'm in need of a speedy dish such as this one. I think the dried Chinese mushrooms have a much earthier flavour than fresh shiitake mushrooms, but it's up to you. Regardless, this is an easy and delicious mushroom egg-fry!

Serves 1 kcal 386 carbs 8.4g protein 15.4g fat 32.6g

Heat a wok over a high heat, add 1 tablespoon of the rapeseed oil and give the oil a swirl. Add the Chinese mushroom slices, season with the tamari or light soy sauce and soft brown sugar and toss, cooking until brown and a little caramelised at the edges. Transfer to a plate.

Wipe out the wok, reheat it to a medium-high heat and add the remaining rapeseed oil. Give the oil a swirl, then crack in the eggs. As the eggs cook for just under 1 minute, lay the mushrooms over the egg whites, then sprinkle with the chives and cook until the bottom of each egg is crispy and the egg yolks are runny. Transfer to a serving plate and drizzle with the vegetarian oyster and sriracha sauces mix.

10 mins

9 mins

Ve GF DF

SAUCY MUSHROOM AND GINGER TOFU

500g fresh firm tofu, drained
   and cut into 2.5cm chunks
pinch of salt
pinch of ground white pepper
½ teaspoon Chinese five-spice
   powder
1 tablespoon tamari or low-
   sodium light soy sauce
1 tablespoon cornflour or potato
   flour
1 tablespoon groundnut oil
2.5cm piece of fresh ginger,
   peeled and sliced into
   matchsticks
5 large dried Chinese
   mushrooms, soaked in hot
   water for 20 minutes, drained,
   stalks discarded, cut into
   crescent slices
1 tablespoon Shaohsing rice wine
   or dry sherry
2 large spring onions, sliced on
   the angle into 2.5cm pieces

For the sauce
1 tablespoon tamari or light soy
   sauce
1 tablespoon vegetarian oyster
   sauce
1 tablespoon chilli sauce
100ml cold vegetable stock
1 tablespoon cornflour

This is one of my own flavour combinations – vegetarian oyster sauce with mushrooms! It's inspired by southern Chinese-style dishes from regions such as Canton and Fujian. So good, and vegan too. Sometimes, I add some baby pak choy in there for extra veg, it's up to you. Wok on! And yes, you guessed it – serve with jasmine rice!

Serves 2 kcal 378 carbs 31.2g protein 25.6g fat 17g

Place the tofu in a bowl and season with the salt, white pepper, five-spice powder and tamari or light soy sauce. Dust with the cornflour or potato flour and toss to mix.

Put all the sauce ingredients into another smaller bowl and stir to mix well.

Heat a wok over a high heat and when the wok starts to smoke, add the groundnut oil. Add the ginger and mushrooms and stir-fry for a few seconds. Then add the tofu pieces and stir-fry for 2–3 minutes, tossing gently for even cooking. Add the rice wine or dry sherry and stir-fry for another 2 minutes, then add the sauce and bring to the boil. Stir-fry for 1 minute, then stir in the spring onions. Remove from the heat and serve immediately.

5 mins

5 mins

Ve GF DF

WOK-FRIED COURGETTES WITH SWEETCORN AND CHILLI

2 tablespoons rapeseed oil

2.5cm piece of fresh ginger, peeled and grated

200g baby courgettes, cut on the angle into 5mm slices

3 tablespoons Shaohsing rice wine or dry sherry

2 small jalapeño chillies, deseeded and finely chopped

2 whole sweetcorn, kernels sliced off

2 tablespoons tamari or low-sodium light soy sauce

1 tablespoon clear rice vinegar

dash of chilli oil

1 tablespoon toasted sesame oil

1 large spring onion, finely sliced, to garnish (optional)

This super delicious dish makes a quick and easy vegan mid-week supper. The sauce the vegetables are wokked in and the pops of pure sweetness from the sweetcorn, make this heavenly. Perfect with brown or jasmine rice.

Serves 2 kcal 280 carbs 16.2g protein 7.2g fat 21g

Heat a wok over a high heat until smoking, add the rapeseed oil and give the oil a swirl. Add the ginger and very quickly stir-fry for a few seconds. Then add the courgettes and toss for 1 minute. Add the rice wine or dry sherry and, if you're cooking on gas, try to catch the flame by tilting the wok (be careful when doing this).

Add the chillies and sweetcorn and stir-fry for 1 minute. Then add the tamari or light soy sauce, vinegar, chilli oil and sesame oil and cook for another minute until all the sweetcorn kernels have softened and turned a richer yellow. Give it a final stir, then transfer to a serving dish. Garnish with the spring onion, if you like, and serve with brown or jasmine rice.

MOCK CHICKEN AND BROCCOLI 'OYSTER' SAUCE CHOW MEIN

1 tablespoon rapeseed oil

3 garlic cloves, finely chopped

2.5cm piece of fresh ginger, peeled and grated

1 red cayenne chilli, sliced (deseeded, if you like)

200g vegetarian mock chicken, cut into strips

1 tablespoon Shaohsing rice wine or dry sherry

250g tenderstem broccoli, sliced on the angle into 2.5cm pieces

1 tablespoon dark soy sauce

400g cooked egg-free noodles of your choice

large handful of beansprouts

2 tablespoons tamari or low-sodium light soy sauce

1 tablespoon vegetarian oyster sauce

One of my favourite vegan suppers, this is ready in minutes. Use noodles of your choice in this one – I tend to go for thin wheat flour noodles or chunky udon noodles, depending on my mood. Children love this dish and it's a great way to get them to eat broccoli.

Serves 2 kcal 576 carbs 89.4g protein 30.4g fat 11.6g

Heat a wok over a high heat until smoking, add the rapeseed oil and give the oil a swirl. Quickly add the garlic, ginger and chilli and stir-fry for a few seconds. Add the mock chicken and stir-fry together for a few seconds.

As the mock chicken starts to brown at the edges, add the rice wine or dry sherry and follow quickly with the broccoli. Stir-fry for 30 seconds, then add the dark soy sauce and toss well.

Add the cooked noodles and give it a good mix, then add the beansprouts. Toss together, then season with the tamari or light soy sauce and vegetarian oyster sauce and cook, tossing and stirring, for less than 1 minute. Serve immediately.

5 mins

9 mins

Ve DF

SICHUAN CHILLI TOMATO MOCK CHICKEN

1 tablespoon groundnut oil

2 garlic cloves, crushed

1 tablespoon roughly sliced, peeled fresh ginger

1 red chilli, deseeded and finely chopped

1 tablespoon Sichuan peppercorns

1 tablespoon chilli bean paste

350g mock chicken, cut into 1cm strips

1 tablespoon Shaohsing rice wine or dry sherry

2 large, ripe heirloom tomatoes, skin on and each quartered (see tip)

2 spring onions, sliced on the angle into 2.5cm lengths

For the sauce

1 tablespoon tamari or light soy sauce

150ml cold vegetable stock

2 tablespoons cornflour

I really like Sichuan peppercorns – their mouthwatering, numbing spice is addictive. Ripe heirloom tomatoes are another favourite, so this is a pairing of two of my favourite ingredients.

Serves 2 kcal 350 carbs 36.2g protein 21g fat 11.6g

Combine all the ingredients for the sauce in a bowl and mix well.

Heat a wok over a high heat and as the wok starts to smoke, add the groundnut oil and give the oil a swirl. Add the garlic, ginger, chilli, Sichuan peppercorns and chilli bean paste and stir well for less than 1 minute. Add the mock chicken and cook for 10 seconds, then add the rice wine or dry sherry and cook for about 1 minute, stirring continuously. Add the tomatoes and stir together.

Add the sauce and bring to the boil, then add the spring onions and cook for 15 seconds. Transfer to serving plates and serve immediately with jasmine rice.

Ching's Tip
No need to peel the tomatoes. The skin holds all the nutrients.

10 mins

5 mins

Ve DF

SICHUAN MOCK CHICKEN AND COURGETTE STIR-FRY

1 tablespoon rapeseed oil

2 small garlic cloves, roughly
chopped

2.5cm piece of fresh ginger,
peeled and finely grated

1 large red cayenne chilli,
deseeded and sliced

200g baby courgettes, cut on
the angle into 5cm slices

200g mock chicken, sliced into
5cm slices

For the Sichuan spicy sauce

1 tablespoon chilli bean paste

2 tablespoons Chinkiang black
rice vinegar or balsamic
vinegar

1 tablespoon tamari or low-
sodium light soy

1 teaspoon soft brown sugar

1 tablespoon cornflour

1 tablespoon Shaohsing rice wine
or dry sherry

1 teaspoon toasted sesame oil

My go-to recipe time and again, this is a quick and easy
vegan stir-fry that is ready in a matter of minutes. Mock
chicken – fried wheat gluten – can be bought from Chinese
supermarkets or you can use a chunky vegan soy protein of
your choice. Serve with steamed jasmine rice.

Serves 2 kcal 306 carbs 27g protein 18g fat 11.8g

Combine all the ingredients for the sauce in a bowl and mix well.

Heat a wok over a high heat until smoking, add the rapeseed
oil and give the oil a swirl. Add the garlic, ginger, chilli and
courgettes and toss for 1 minute, then add a small splash of cold
water around the edge of the wok to help create some steam.
Add the mock chicken and toss together for 30 seconds until it
is warmed through.

Pour in the sauce and bring to the boil and coat the ingredients
well. Then give the dish a final stir, take it off the heat and serve
immediately with steamed rice.

10 mins

6 mins

Ve GF DF

FRIED TOFU AND BABY PAK CHOY IN VEGETARIAN OYSTER SAUCE

2 tablespoons groundnut oil

2 garlic cloves, roughly chopped

2.5cm piece of fresh ginger, peeled and grated

1 red cayenne chilli, deseed one half and leave seeds in the other half, sliced

200g firm tofu pieces, sliced into 2.5cm chunks

350g baby pak choy, leaves separated

small handful of shimeji mushrooms, trimmed

2 tablespoons vegetarian oyster sauce

1 tablespoon Shaohsing rice wine or dry sherry

1 teaspoon dark soy sauce

1 tablespoon tamari or low-sodium light soy sauce

1 tablespoon clear rice vinegar

1 tablespoon toasted sesame oil

1 large spring onion, greens sliced, to garnish

This is a variation of my favourite saucy stir-fry, though this is more of a dry-fry. It makes a healthy dinner in minutes and is perfect with an array of other dishes to share or to have on its own with noodles or rice.

Serves 2 kcal 310 carbs 14.2g protein 13.8g fat 21.4g

Heat a wok over a high heat until smoking, add the groundnut oil and give the oil a swirl. Add the garlic, ginger and chilli and stir-fry for a few seconds, then add the tofu. Cook, stirring, for less than 1 minute, then add the pak choy leaves. Toss for a few seconds, then add the mushrooms and a few splashes of cold water around the edge of the wok to create some steam to help the vegetables cook.

Make a well in the centre of the vegetables and season with the vegetarian oyster sauce, the rice wine or dry sherry, the dark soy sauce, tamari or light soy sauce and vinegar, then toss the vegetables to coat them well.

Lastly, season with the sesame oil and take off the heat. Transfer to a serving dish, garnish with the spring onion and serve with steamed jasmine rice.

5 mins

2–3 mins

Ve DF

SPICED MOCK CHICKEN WITH MANGETOUT AND SUGARSNAP PEAS

1 tablespoon rapeseed oil

2.5cm piece of fresh ginger, peeled and grated

150g sugarsnap peas

150g mangetout, sliced in half if they are large

200g mock chicken, cut into strips

1 teaspoon chilli bean paste

1 teaspoon tamari or low-sodium light soy sauce

pinch of soft brown sugar

4 tablespoons roasted salted cashew nuts

A simple stir-fry of sugarsnap peas and mangetout with cashew nuts, this can be served as a side dish or as a meal for two. If you are watching your salt intake, use raw cashew nuts rather than salted. Chilli bean paste is available from good Chinese grocers and online, but if you can't get it leave it out.

Serves 2 kcal 337 carbs 16.9g protein 17.7g fat 18.8g

Heat a wok over a high heat until smoking, add the rapeseed oil and give it a swirl. Add the ginger and allow to sizzle for 30 seconds, then add the sugarsnap peas and mangetout and stir-fry for 1–2 minutes. Add the mock chicken and season with the chilli bean paste, light soy sauce and brown sugar. Toss well, then sprinkle in the cashews and serve immediately.

10 mins

7 mins

Ve DF

SICHUAN SPICY SALT AND PEPPER MOCK DUCK

300g jasmine rice, rinsed until water runs clear

350g mock duck, cut into 1cm strips

few pinches of ground white pepper

1 tablespoon cornflour or potato flour

2 tablespoons rapeseed oil

1 tablespoon mirin

1 teaspoon Sichuan peppercorns, crushed

bunch of spring onions, cut into 5cm pieces (optional)

2 tablespoons tamari or low-sodium light soy sauce

few pinches each of salt and cracked black pepper

2 teaspoons chilli oil

juice of 1 lime

2 teaspoons toasted sesame seeds

1 red chilli, deseeded and finely chopped, to garnish

This is a stir-fry dish inspired by Sichuan in China. The hot chilli and spices warm the senses and make an elegant, quick and inexpensive dish for entertaining when served with plain rice. Spring onions are the choice of veg here, but if you don't like them, substitute with a veg of your choice.

Serves 4 kcal 454 carbs 74.4g protein 18.1g fat 11.2g

Place the rice in a medium pan, add 500ml water and bring to the boil. Turn the heat to low, put the lid on and keep on a gentle simmer for 20 minutes until the grains are cooked, then fluff with a fork.

Meanwhile, season the mock duck with a few pinches of salt, the white pepper and cornflour or potato flour.

Heat a wok over a high heat until smoking, add the rapeseed oil and give the oil a swirl. Add the mock duck pieces and stir-fry for 1 minute. Deglaze the wok with the mirin. Add the Sichuan peppercorns and spring onions, if using, and toss all together, stirring for 20 seconds. Add the tamari or light soy sauce and season with a few pinches of salt and black pepper. Stir in the chilli oil, lime juice and toasted sesame seeds. Transfer to serving plates, garnish with the chilli and serve immediately with the rice.

10 mins

5 mins

V GF DF

EGGY TOMATO CABBAGE HO FUN

3 eggs

1 tablespoon cornflour, blended with 2 tablespoons cold water

1 tablespoon rapeseed oil

2 garlic cloves, grated

2 red chillies, deseeded and finely chopped

¼ white cabbage, finely shredded

3 large ripe tomatoes, quartered

100g canned chopped tomatoes

1 tablespoon Shaohsing rice wine or dry sherry

50ml vegetable stock

150g dried pad Thai rice noodles, soaked in warm water for 10 minutes, drained

2 tablespoons tamari or low-sodium light soy sauce

2 spring onions, finely sliced on the angle, to garnish

This is an eggy, tomatoey, delicious veggie stir-fry, perfect for adults and kids alike. It's pure comfort food and great for a snack or dinner. For an extra kick, serve with some sriracha chilli sauce. For vegans, lose the eggs and instead add meaty shiitake mushrooms and more spring onions.

Serves 2 kcal 563 carbs 90.7g protein 22.6g fat 14.2g

Beat the eggs in a small bowl, then stir in the blended cornflour.

Heat a wok over a high heat until smoking, add the rapeseed oil and give it a swirl. Add the garlic and chillies and stir-fry for a few seconds to release their aroma. Add the cabbage and stir-fry for 30 seconds. Add the fresh tomatoes and wok-fry for 10 seconds, then add the canned tomatoes and season the mixture with the rice wine or dry sherry. Add the vegetable stock and, as the sauce starts to reduce, quickly add the noodles and toss for 30 seconds.

Make a well in the centre of the mixture, pour in the beaten egg mixture and mix together to scramble. Toss all the ingredients together, season with the tamari or light soy sauce, garnish with the spring onions and serve immediately.

Ve GF DF

SOY BEANSPROUT CORIANDER CHEUNG FUN ROLLS

2 tablespoons rapeseed oil
400g fresh cheung fun rice
    noodle rolls (cigar-shaped,
    about 1cm thick) or pre-soaked
    pad Thai noodles
2 tablespoons tamari or low-
    sodium light soy sauce
2 tablespoons vegetarian oyster
    sauce
200g beansprouts
1 teaspoon toasted sesame oil
pinch of ground white pepper
large handful of coriander,
    roughly chopped

Nothing screams Asian comfort food more than fat cheung fun rice noodle rolls – delicious, silky and perfect when steamed and dressed with a sweet soy sauce. However, I like mine wok-fried in a good-quality soy sauce, with some crunchy beansprouts and chopped coriander. Simple and moreish. If you can't get cheung fun rolls (usually found in the fresh section of Chinese supermarkets), go for dried, flat, wide rice noodles like pad Thai noodles. It won't be the same experience, but it will still be delicious. This is a favourite with my vegan friends too.

Serves 2 kcal 526 carbs 83.8g protein 9.8g fat 18.2g

Heat a wok over a high heat until smoking, add the rapeseed oil and give the oil a swirl. Add the noodle rolls and wok-fry for 20 seconds, then season with the tamari or light soy sauce. Add the vegetarian oyster sauce and beansprouts and toss for a few seconds to mix well. Season with the sesame oil and white pepper, then stir in the chopped coriander and eat immediately.

5 mins

3 mins

Ve GF DF

WOK-FRIED GINGER SOY PAK CHOY WITH CRISPY SHALLOTS

1 tablespoon rapeseed oil
pinch of salt flakes
1 teaspoon grated peeled fresh
   ginger
200g baby pak choy, each head
   quartered
1 tablespoon Shaohsing rice wine
   or dry sherry
1 teaspoon Chinkiang black rice
   vinegar or balsamic vinegar
1 teaspoon tamari or low-sodium
   light soy sauce
½ teaspoon cornflour, blended
   with 1 teaspoon cold water
½ teaspoon toasted sesame oil
small handful of deep-fried
   sliced shallots, to garnish
   (optional)

One of my all-time favourite go-to vegetable dishes. Pak choy, which translates as 'white vegetable', belongs to the same family as the cabbage and has two types – white-stemmed and green-stemmed. Both are equally delicious when wokked up in this way.

Serves 2 kcal 146 carbs 9.1g protein 2.3g fat 11g

Heat a wok over a high heat until smoking, add the rapeseed oil and give the oil a swirl. Season the oil with the salt, then add the ginger and stir-fry for a couple of seconds. Add the pak choy and toss for less than 1 minute. Season with the rice wine or dry sherry, the vinegar and tamari or light soy sauce, then drizzle in the blended cornflour. Add the sesame oil and give it one last toss. Pour out onto serving plates, garnish with some crushed fried shallots, if you like, and serve immediately.

10 mins

5 mins

Ve GF DF

MOREISH CRISPY SEAWEED

sunflower oil, for deep-frying
200g pak choy, stems removed,
    finely shredded
pinches of salt, to taste
pinches of granulated sugar,
    to taste
1 tablespoon toasted sesame
    seeds, to garnish

This is not served in China but is a Western Chinese dish invented by Chinese cooks. It doesn't actually contain seaweed but is made with finely shredded pak choy leaves that are deep-fried. I like to season mine with salt and granulated sugar so that it's both sweet and salty.

It's a great way to use up any leftover pak choy you have that may have wilted. If you're neither vegan nor vegetarian, this is also great as an appetiser or sprinkled as a garnish over crispy squid.

Serves 4 kcal 48 carbs 1.2g protein 1.2g fat 4.1g

Heat a wok over a high heat. Fill the wok to a third of its depth with the oil and heat to 180°C. Add half the pak choy leaves and deep-fry for a few seconds, then lift out using a spider and drain on kitchen paper. Cook the rest of the pak choy in the same way. Season the seaweed with salt and sugar, transfer to a serving dish and sprinkle on some toasted sesame seeds. Serve immediately.

10 mins

8 mins

V DF GF

JAPANESE RICE OMELETTE (OMU-RAISU)

For the rice filling
1 tablespoon rapeseed oil
1 small white onion, diced
50g smoked tofu, sliced
½ red pepper, deseeded and
    diced
½ green pepper, deseeded and
    diced
4 white mushrooms, diced
350g cooked jasmine rice
3 tablespoons tomato ketchup
1 tablespoon tamari or low-
    sodium light soy sauce
pinch of salt
pinch of ground white pepper

For the omelettes (makes 2)
2 tablespoons rapeseed oil
6 eggs
2 pinches each of salt and
    ground white pepper

To serve
sriracha chilli sauce
mixed salad leaves or cos lettuce
    leaves

Rice is truly versatile – it can be stir-fried, cooked in a soup, steamed and made into rice parcel dumplings; and, of course, it's an accompaniment for curries too. In this easy-to-make and quick Japanese snack, rice accompanies eggs to make a delicious rice omelette.

Serves 2 kcal 692 carbs 63.1g protein 33.2g fat 36g

Heat a wok over a high heat until smoking, add the rapeseed oil and give the oil a swirl. Add the onion and wok-fry for 15 seconds until golden and translucent, then add the smoked tofu and stir-fry for 30 seconds. Add the red and green peppers and the mushrooms and stir-fry for another minute. Tip in the cooked rice and stir-fry for another minute.

Season with the tomato ketchup, tamari or light soy sauce, salt and white pepper. Transfer to an ovenproof dish and keep covered in the oven on a low heat.

To make the omelettes, wipe the wok with kitchen paper, then reheat over a medium heat, add half the rapeseed oil and give the oil a swirl. Beat three of the eggs, add a pinch of salt and white pepper and spread the egg in an even layer in the wok. When the omelette is almost cooked, place half the fried rice on one half and fold the omelette over the rice. Keep covered and warm in the low oven while you repeat with the remaining oil, eggs, seasoning and rice.

Serve the omelettes with a side of sriracha chilli sauce and some mixed salad leaves or cos lettuce leaves.

8 mins

6 mins

Ve GF DF

VEGGIE 'PORK' MINCE WITH FRENCH BEANS

1 tablespoon rapeseed oil

2 garlic cloves, finely chopped

1 red chilli, deseeded and finely chopped

300g rehydrated soy textured protein mince

½ teaspoon Chinese five-spice powder

1 teaspoon dark soy sauce

1 tablespoon Shaohsing rice wine or dry sherry

150g French beans, sliced on the angle into 3cm pieces

50ml cold vegetable stock

1 tablespoon tamari or low-sodium light soy sauce

1 tablespoon Chinkiang black rice vinegar or balsamic vinegar

1 teaspoon cornflour, blended with 1 tablespoon cold water

pinch of ground white pepper

1 teaspoon toasted sesame oil

½ teaspoon chilli oil

handful of coriander, to garnish

This is such a satisfying vegan supper. Textured veggie protein mince is made from soy beans and makes a delicious meaty substitute. Some come dried and others already rehydrated (like Quorn mince). I use the Clearspring brand, which is dried, so you need to follow the packet instructions to rehydrate it. French beans are super sweet and crunchy – a great veg for all year round. Perfect on rice or noodles.

Serves 2 kcal 514 carbs 25.5g protein 67.4g fat 16.5g

Heat a wok over a high heat until smoking, add the rapeseed oil and give the oil a swirl. Add the garlic and chilli and toss for a few seconds to release their flavours. Add the soy mince and let it settle in the wok for 30 seconds to brown and sear, then stir-fry for 1 minute. Add the five-spice powder and season with the dark soy sauce. Toss until the mince turns a rich brown colour, then season and deglaze the wok with the rice wine or dry sherry.

Add the French beans and toss for 2 minutes. Pour in the vegetable stock and bring to the boil, then season with the tamari or light soy sauce and vinegar. Stir in the blended cornflour to give the dish a shine, then add a pinch of white pepper. Season with the toasted sesame oil and chilli oil and garnish with the coriander before serving.

CLASSIC PLAIN CONGEE 'ZHOU'

250g uncooked jasmine rice
50g glutinous rice (optional)
250ml vegetable stock
salt (optional)

Although in my family congee is eaten mainly for breakfast or lunch, it can also be eaten at dinner time. Congee mainly consists of two types of rice – short-grain and some glutinous rice for a stickier, thicker consistency. If you have some glutinous rice in your cupboard then by all means add 50g of it to the recipe, otherwise leave it out. This is, of course, a more classic congee, where it is very slowly cooked on the stove. For a cheat and speedy congee, see page 187. To make it vegan, just substitute the beef with tofu strips or mock duck pieces instead.

If you like, you can add cooked mung beans and split yellow beans in with the cooked congee at the end. Whenever I had an upset stomach, my grandmother would give me a steaming bowl of salted congee and I would feel like I would live to see another day!

Serves 4 kcal 237 carbs 56.4g protein 5.3g fat 0.6g

Place all the rice in a sieve and wash under cold running water until the water runs clear. Drain well and pour into a large wok.

Add 700ml water and the vegetable stock and bring to the boil over a high heat. Once boiling, turn the heat to medium, put a lid on top of the wok and cook for 1 hour, stirring occasionally to make sure the rice does not stick to the side and bottom of the wok. Cook until it forms a thick rice porridge. If you prefer a much more watery consistency, add more hot water. Serve as an accompaniment.

Ching's Tip
Add salt if you have a stomach ache – trust me: it's an age-old remedy and it works!

8 mins

+ 20 minutes soaking for
dried Chinese mushrooms

3 mins

Ve DF

MOCK PORK CONGEE

1 tablespoon rapeseed oil

2 shallots, finely diced

4 dried Chinese mushrooms,
soaked in hot water for 20
minutes, drained and diced

150g vegetarian mock pork,
diced

2 celery sticks, finely diced

2 tablespoons tamari or low-
sodium light soy sauce

1 quantity cooked Classic Plain
Congee 'Zhou' (see opposite)

pinch of salt

pinch of ground white pepper

1 tablespoon toasted sesame oil

2 dried nori sheets, shredded

1 spring onion, finely chopped

I love Chinese 'ham' or 'shu-rou' (plant/tree meat) as we call it
in Mandarin. If you can't get it, vegetarian mock pork is equally
good and delicious.

The mix of textures here is great – the chewiness of the earthy
Chinese mushrooms, the crunchy texture of the celery and
the bite of the seaweed. Like Marmite, this is one that you will
either love or hate.

Serves 2 kcal 420 carbs 48g protein 22.3g fat 16.8g

Heat a wok over a high heat until smoking, add the rapeseed oil
and give it a swirl. Add the shallots and stir-fry for 1 minute until
translucent. Add the Chinese mushrooms, mock pork and celery
and stir-fry for 2 minutes until aromatic, then season with the
soy sauce.

Add this to the cooked congee and stir in well. Season with the
salt, white pepper and toasted sesame oil. Stir in the shredded
nori, add the spring onion and serve immediately.

SPICED VEGAN LARB LETTUCE CUPS

1 tablespoon rapeseed oil
200g soy textured protein mince
1 fresh kaffir lime leaf, very finely
    sliced into strips, or zest of 1 lime
1 tablespoon tamari or low-
    sodium light soy sauce
pinch of ground white pepper
pinch of dried chilli flakes
juice of ½ lime

For the spice mixture

1 teaspoon ground Sichuan
    peppercorns
1 teaspoon ground cumin powder
¼ teaspoon ground cloves
1 teaspoon vegetable bouillon
    powder
¼ teaspoon ground star anise
1 teaspoon ground jasmine rice
1 teaspoon dried chilli flakes

To assemble

1 small cucumber, cut on a deep
    angle into 3mm slices
hoisin sauce, for dipping
2-3 Little Gem lettuces, leaves
    separated from the stalks
1 small carrot, cut into julienne
    strips
5g chives, snipped into pieces
1 lime, quartered

This Chinese-Laos dish is a spiced vegetable stir-fry using soy textured protein mince as the meat substitute and some aromatic seasonings, then served in fresh, crunchy, Little Gem lettuce cups. It is my vegan version of 'spiced larb'. Make a large batch of the spice mix and then store the rest in a small glass jar to use on another occasion. It may seem like a long list of ingredients, but I promise you'll find most in your store cupboard. This makes a delicious starter or you can turn it into a main dish – I often like to tear the lettuce into pieces, then pour the hot spiced stir-fry over it and eat it like a hot/cold salad. Delicious.

Serves 4 kcal 189 carbs 10.5g protein 24.4g fat 6.7g

Toast all the ingredients for the spice mixture in a dry wok until fragrant, then place in a pestle and mortar (or use a clean coffee grinder) and grind to mix.

Heat a wok over a high heat until smoking, add the rapeseed oil and give it a swirl. Add 1 teaspoon of the spice mixture and toast for a few seconds, then add the soy textured protein mince and wok-fry together until dry, crisp and golden. Add the kaffir lime strips or lime zest and season with the tamari or light soy sauce, the white pepper, chilli flakes and lime juice.

To assemble a lettuce cup, dip a few cucumber slices in some hoisin sauce, place in a lettuce leaf, top with a couple of carrot strips, then with some spiced vegan 'larb' and chives and eat immediately, served with the lime wedges on the side. You can assemble the individual cups, or I like to serve all the elements separately and let everyone build their own.

VEGAN PHO

2.5cm piece of fresh ginger,
    peeled and left whole
2 stalks of lemongrass, sliced
3 red onions, halved
2 small carrots, sliced on the
    angle into 1cm slices
8 cherry tomatoes
100g Chinese leaf, sliced
2 tablespoons vegetable bouillon
    powder
1 star anise
100g mixed fresh mushrooms –
    shiitake, enoki, oyster
100g fresh corn cobs, sliced in
    2.5cm rounds
2 x 100g blocks dried instant
    vermicelli rice noodles or flat
    rice noodles
1 teaspoon sriracha chilli sauce
large pinch of salt
large pinch of ground white
    pepper
juice of 2 limes
100g fried tofu slices or smoked
    tofu slices
100g beansprouts
1 spring onion, sliced

For the garnish and to serve
handful each of Thai basil, mint
    and coriander leaves
1 red chilli, deseeded and sliced
sriracha chilli sauce

This is clean, refreshing and restorative, and uses a basic
'cheat' pho broth. You can add as much spice to it as you like
and vary the vegetables. I could eat it any time of the year.

If using flat rice noodles, soak them in warm water for
5 minutes, then drain.

Serves 2 kcal 428 carbs 71.7g protein 18.5g fat 8.2g

Heat a wok over a medium heat, add the ginger, lemongrass, red
onions and carrots and char-brown for 1–2 minutes. Then add 1.2
litres water, the tomatoes, Chinese leaf, bouillon powder and star
anise and simmer for 5 minutes until the Chinese leaves have
wilted and the tomatoes have softened and are ready to burst.

Add the mushrooms, corn and noodles and simmer for 1–2
minutes.

Season with the chilli sauce, salt, white pepper and lime juice
and stir in well. Stir in the tofu slices and beansprouts and
sprinkle the spring onion over.

Divide into two bowls and garnish with the basil, mint and coriander
leaves and the chilli slices. Serve with sriracha on the side.

VEGAN SQUASH, TURNIP AND CARROT BROTH WITH CORIANDER

2 tablespoons vegetable bouillon powder
250g squash flesh, cut into 2.5cm pieces, blanched and drained
2.5cm piece of fresh ginger, peeled and sliced into matchsticks
200g daikon, sliced into 1cm rounds, then each cut into 6 wedges
2 carrots, cut into 1cm rounds and then quartered to give wedges
1 tablespoon Shaohsing rice wine or dry sherry
pinch of salt
pinch of ground white pepper
handful of roughly chopped coriander leaves

This is one of my grandfather's favourite recipes. The light, sweet broth is not overpowering and the daikon adds a slight bitter-sweetness. The coriander adds an aromatic fragrance at the end. It reminds me of my grandmother's home-style cooking. I hope you like this as much as I do. It's perfect for a light supper and is super healthy too.

Serves 4 kcal 62 carbs 11.8g protein 2.2g fat 0.9g

Bring 1.5 litres water to the boil in a wok, then stir in the bouillon powder until dissolved. Add the squash, ginger, daikon, carrots and rice wine or dry sherry and simmer over a low heat for 20 minutes until the squash, daikon and carrots are tender. Season with the salt and white pepper. Just before serving, add the chopped coriander and serve immediately. Perfect spooned over cooked jasmine rice for a delicious rice soup.

20 mins

10 mins

Ve GF DF

VEGAN GOLDEN SPICED TURMERIC TOFU WITH ASPARAGUS, SHIITAKE AND CHICKPEA FRIED RICE

For the fried rice
300g brown rice
300ml vegetable stock
200g can chickpeas, drained and
    rinsed

For the turmeric tofu
400g block of fresh firm tofu,
    drained, cut into 1.5cm squares
pinch of salt
pinch of ground white pepper
pinch each of ground turmeric,
    dried chilli flakes, ground
    cumin, ground fennel
1 tablespoon cornflour
2 tablespoons rapeseed oil

For the vegetables
1 tablespoon rapeseed oil
1 garlic clove, finely chopped
1 teaspoon finely grated peeled
    fresh ginger
1 red chilli, deseeded and finely
    chopped
1 small carrot, finely diced
50g asparagus spears, diced
6 fresh shiitake mushrooms,
    stems discarded, sliced
2 tablespoons tamari or low-
    sodium light soy sauce
2 tablespoons vegetarian oyster
    sauce
1 teaspoon toasted sesame oil

For the garnish
1 spring onion, finely chopped
small handful of coriander
    leaves, chopped

If you are vegan, this rice dish will hopefully send you to heaven!

Serves 4 kcal 511 carbs 75.6g protein 19.8g fat 16.2g

Wash the rice until the water runs clear, place with the stock and 350ml water in a medium pan, bring to the boil, then turn the heat down to low, cover with a lid, and cook for 15 minutes. Pour in the chickpeas and stir, then cover and keep warm until ready to stir-fry.

Place the tofu pieces in a shallow bowl, sprinkle with the salt, white pepper, turmeric, chilli flakes, cumin, fennel and cornflour and turn gently to coat.

Heat a wok over a medium heat, add the rapeseed oil and give the oil a swirl. Add the tofu and wok-fry on each side for 2 minutes until seared and golden, using a flat knife or spatula to help you turn the tofu gently without breaking up the pieces. Transfer to a warm plate, cover and keep in an oven set to low heat until ready to serve.

For the vegetables, clean the wok and reheat over a high heat until smoking. Add the rapeseed oil and swirl the oil around, then add the garlic, ginger and chilli and stir for a few seconds until fragrant. Add the diced carrot and stir for 2 minutes or until tender. Toss in the asparagus and shiitake mushrooms and stir-fry for another minute. Season with the tamari or light soy sauce, vegetarian oyster sauce and the sesame oil and stir well. Toss the chickpea rice in and mix well. Adjust the seasoning, adding more soy, vegetarian oyster sauce to taste. Top with the turmeric tofu, garnish with the spring onion and coriander and serve.

3 mins

8 mins

V DF

CANTONESE-STYLE EGG AND TOMATO MACARONI NOODLE SOUP

3 ripe tomatoes, sliced

1 tablespoon vegetable bouillon powder

200g canned plum tomatoes, retain juices from the can

3 eggs, lightly beaten

1 tablespoon tamari or low-sodium light soy sauce

dash of toasted sesame oil

pinch of salt

pinch of ground white pepper

1 tablespoon sriracha chilli sauce, to taste

300g cooked macaroni pasta, drained, dressed in a little rapeseed oil

1 tablespoon cornflour, blended with 2 tablespoons cold water

large handful of baby spinach (optional)

2 spring onions, finely sliced

A classic comfort dish served in many of the licensed street vendors (dai pai dongs) offering Hong Kongers a quick snack. Add a good amount of sriracha for a kicked-up version. This is pure comfort in a bowl and yes, you read correctly, you'll want canned plum tomatoes for a rich tart flavour.

Serves 2 kcal 473 carbs 75.3g protein 22.8g fat 11g

If you want to skin the fresh tomatoes before chopping, cut a small cross at the base of each one. Plunge them into a wok or pan of boiling water for less than 1 minute, then drain. The skin will peel off easily. Finely chop the flesh, discarding the hard centre. However, most of the nutrients are underneath the skin so I don't bother – also it does make the dish even quicker to prepare.

Pour 800ml boiling water into a wok and bring back to the boil. Stir in the bouillon powder and bring to a simmer, then add the fresh tomatoes and cook over a medium heat for 5 minutes until the tomatoes have softened. Add the canned plum tomatoes with their juices and bring to a simmer. Pour the beaten eggs into the broth, stirring gently. Add the tamari or light soy sauce, sesame oil, salt, white pepper, sriracha chilli sauce, cooked macaroni and blended cornflour. Mix well and heat through. If using, add the baby spinach and let it wilt, then garnish with the spring onions and serve immediately.

+ 20 mins to soak
wood ear mushrooms

15 mins

Ve GF DF

VEGAN TRADITIONAL HOT AND SOUR SOUP

1 tablespoon vegetable bouillon
    powder
1 tablespoon grated peeled fresh
    ginger
2 chillies, deseeded and finely
    chopped
1 teaspoon Shaohsing rice wine
    or dry sherry
1 tablespoon dark soy sauce
200g Chinese leaf, shredded
220g can bamboo shoots, drained
    and cut into julienne strips
10g dried wood ear mushrooms,
    soaked in hot water for 20
    minutes, drained and finely
    sliced
100g fresh firm tofu, drained, cut
    into 5cm long x 1cm wide strips
50g Sichuan preserved
    vegetables in chilli oil, rinsed
    and sliced (optional)
2 tablespoons tamari or low-
    sodium light soy sauce
3 tablespoons Chinkiang black
    rice vinegar or balsamic vinegar
1 tablespoon chilli oil
2 pinches of ground white pepper
1 tablespoon cornflour, blended
    with 2 tablespoons cold water
100g enoki mushrooms, root
    ends discarded, cut into 2.5cm
    slices
1 large spring onion, finely sliced
handful of chopped coriander,
    to serve

The spicy chillies, the sourness of the earthy black rice vinegar, the softness of the tofu and the crunchy wood ear mushrooms and bamboo shoots make this one of my all-time favourite soup recipes – and the best thing is that it's my husband's favourite too, so whenever I get into trouble with him, all is forgiven if I make this. It may look like a long list of ingredients, but trust me, it's a one-wok situation and everything goes in. To make it into a more substantial meal, just add noodles or pour onto steamed rice.

Serves 4 kcal 128 carbs 15.6g protein 5.8g fat 4.8g

Pour 1 litre water into a wok and bring to the boil. Add the bouillon powder and stir to dissolve. Bring back to the boil, then add all the ingredients up to the tofu, including the wood ear mushrooms. Boil for 3 minutes, then turn the heat down to medium and add the tofu, preserved vegetables (or leave out if you don't have any), tamari or light soy sauce. vinegar, chilli oil and white pepper and simmer for 10 minutes.

Stir in the blended cornflour to thicken the soup (add more if you like a thicker consistency). Drop in the enoki mushrooms, spring onion and coriander and serve immediately.

20 mins

+ 1 hour marinating

10 mins

Ve DF

VEGAN CRISPY 'BOTTOM' 'GUO TIEH' VEGETABLE DUMPLINGS

100g carrots, finely diced

100g dried shiitake mushrooms, soaked in hot water for 20 minutes, drained and finely chopped

160g smoked tofu

1 teaspoon salt

¼ teaspoon ground white pepper

½ teaspoon caster sugar

½ vegetable stock cube, grated

¼ teaspoon toasted sesame oil

¼ teaspoon light soy sauce

¼ teaspoon Shaohsing rice wine or dry sherry

2.5cm piece of fresh ginger, peeled and grated

120g Chinese leaf, finely diced

40g spring onions, finely diced

80g canned water chestnuts, drained and finely diced

1 tablespoon cornflour

1 packet (30) wheat-flour gyoza dumpling wrappers

1 tablespoon rapeseed oil

1 tablespoon plain flour

30g chives, to garnish

*per dumpling

These Cantonese-style pot-stickers are perfect party food. You can leave them in the pan and keep covered warm until ready to serve, or you can serve them straight from the pan.

Makes 30 kcal 48 carbs 8.1g protein 2g fat 1.1g*

Mix the carrots, mushrooms and tofu with the salt, white pepper, sugar, grated stock cube, sesame oil, soy sauce, rice wine or dry sherry and grated ginger. Add the Chinese leaf, spring onions and water chestnuts and use your hands to mix thoroughly. Cover with clingfilm and leave in the fridge for around 1 hour. Remove the vegetables, drain any excess water and stir in the cornflour.

Place a dumpling wrapper in your palm and put 2 generous teaspoons of the filling in the middle. Gently bring one half of the dumpling sheet over the other half and squeeze the edges. To make the dumpling more decorative, add some folds around the edges. Continue until the remaining 29 dumpling wrappers are filled.

Heat a wok over a low heat, add the rapeseed oil and give it a swirl. Arrange the dumplings in the wok, cover (see tip) and cook for 2 minutes.

Put the flour in a jug, add around 250ml water and mix until most lumps are gone. Pour over the frying dumplings, turn the heat to medium, cover with a lid and cook until the water has evaporated.

Gently remove the dumplings from the wok (the flour-water will turn into a crispy and delicate flour sheet and may break easily when lifting the dumplings out from the pan).

Arrange on a serving plate and garnish each dumpling with 2 chives criss-crossed over the top.

Ching's Tip

A see-through lid is handy, so that you can see, without lifting the lid, when the water has evaporated.

VEGAN 'TOM YUM' (SOUP)

10 mins

8 mins

Ve GF DF

1 tablespoon vegetable bouillon
  powder
1 garlic clove, grated
1 teaspoon freshly grated peeled
  galangal, or freshly grated
  peeled ginger
1 stalk of lemongrass, grated
1 kaffir lime leaf, fresh or dried
1 red chilli, deseeded and finely
  chopped
50g fresh firm tofu, drained and
  sliced into 2cm cubes
4 fresh shiitake mushrooms,
  rinsed, sliced
4 cherry tomatoes
½ head of baby pak choy, leaves
  separated
100ml reduced-fat coconut milk
pinch of soft brown sugar
1 tablespoon tamari or low-
  sodium light soy sauce
juice of 1 lime

To serve
small handful of Thai basil leaves,
  finely shredded
small handful of coriander,
  roughly chopped

A spicy Thai classic, to which I've added a few more ingredients, that is just bursting with flavour. The chilli and ginger not only add wonderful spice notes but also are thermogenic, meaning they speed up the metabolism. The tofu provides protein, iron and calcium and a host of minerals. Shiitake mushrooms are not only delicious, they're also a good source of iron and antioxidants and boost the immune system. A tasty dish that is also fabulous for your health!

Serves 2 kcal 151 carbs 13g protein 8.9g fat 6.5g

Pour 500ml water into a wok and bring to the boil. Add the bouillon powder and stir to dissolve, then add all the ingredients down to and including the chilli. Bring to a gentle simmer and cook for 10 minutes until the broth is infused with their flavours.

Add the tofu and mushrooms and cook for 3 minutes. Then add the tomatoes and simmer for 1–2 minutes.

Reduce the heat to low and add the pak choy, coconut milk, sugar, tamari or light soy sauce and the lime juice. Season to taste to your liking, adding more chillies, lime juice or salt, if you wish.

To serve, ladle the soup into two large bowls and garnish with the basil and coriander.

10 mins

5 mins

Ve GF DF

VEGAN SMOKED TOFU AND HOT AND SOUR COURGETTI NOODLES

2 large courgettes, cut thinly lengthways to make courgetti noodles
100g smoked tofu, cut into julienne strips

For the fragrant hot oil dressing
1 tablespoon rapeseed oil
1 garlic clove, finely chopped
2.5cm piece of fresh ginger, peeled and grated
1 red chilli, deseeded and finely chopped
1 tablespoon tamari or low-sodium light soy sauce
1 tablespoon Chinkiang black rice vinegar or balsamic vinegar
½ tablespoon toasted sesame oil
1 tablespoon Sichuan chilli oil
pinch of ground toasted Sichuan peppercorns
pinch of cracked salt
small handful of chopped coriander

A great low-carb dinner with a spicy kick! The courgetti noodles are full of fibre, the hot oil dressing is super tasty, and the black rice vinegar provides a nice tangy-sour flavour. Children prefer courgetti hot and blanched but you might prefer it uncooked, it's up to you.

Serves 2 kcal 241 carbs 10.3g protein 14.9g fat 15.6g

Pour 500ml water into a medium pan and bring to the boil. Keep on a gentle simmer.

To make the dressing, heat a wok over a high heat until smoking, add the rapeseed oil and give the oil a swirl. Add the garlic, ginger and red chilli and toss for a few seconds, then add the rest of the ingredients. Set aside to keep hot.

Toss the courgette strips into the simmering water for 20 seconds to soften, lift out, drain and add to the wok together with the smoked tofu. Toss it all together well to heat through, then eat immediately.

SWEETCORN MAPO TOFU

15 mins

5 mins

Ve GF DF

1–2 tablespoons peanut oil

2 garlic cloves, finely chopped

2.5cm piece of fresh ginger, peeled and grated

1 red chilli, deseeded and finely chopped

1 teaspoon fermented salted black beans, rinsed and crushed

1 tablespoon chilli bean paste

150g fresh sweetcorn kernels

250g firm fresh tofu, drained, sliced into 2.5cm cubes

1 tablespoon Shaohsing rice wine or dry sherry

1 tablespoon tamari or low-sodium light soy sauce

1 tablespoon Chinkiang black rice vinegar or balsamic vinegar

200ml hot vegetable stock

1 tablespoon Sichuan preserved vegetables in chilli oil, finely chopped

1 tablespoon cornflour, blended with 2 tablespoons cold water

salt and freshly ground pepper, to taste

For the garnish

2 pinches of ground toasted Sichuan peppercorns

1 spring onion, finely sliced

1 small handful of chopped coriander stems, and hand-picked leaves

Spicy mapo tofu was invented by Mrs Chen, a Sichuan street hawker who put the dish and Chengdu on the culinary map! The classic version includes some minced pork and Sichuan preserved vegetables, for that sour briny taste, which I also use in this dish. But I use tofu and have also added some sweetcorn kernels for a sweet modern vegan take! Serve with jasmine rice.

Serves 2 kcal 378 carbs 23.2g protein 17g fat 24.2g

Heat a wok over a high heat and add the peanut oil. Give it a swirl and add the garlic, ginger and chilli. Cook, stirring, for a few seconds, then add the fermented salted black beans and the chilli bean paste, followed by the sweetcorn kernels and tofu, and toss, cooking for 10 seconds.

Add the rice wine or dry sherry, tamari or light soy sauce, vinegar and stock, and bring to the boil. Stir in the Sichuan preserved vegetables and blended cornflour.

Serve immediately with jasmine rice, garnished with the ground toasted Sichuan peppercorns, spring onion and coriander stems and leaves.

10 mins

5 mins

V DF

SICHUAN-STYLE LIANG MIAN

300g dried egg noodles

1 tablespoon toasted sesame oil

For the hot sauce

1 tablespoon rapeseed oil

2 garlic cloves, finely chopped

2.5cm piece of fresh ginger, peeled and grated

1 red chilli, deseeded and finely chopped

1 tablespoon chilli bean paste

1 tablespoon Shaohsing rice wine or dry sherry

2 tablespoons black sesame paste or tahini

50ml hot vegetable stock

2–3 tablespoons tamari or low-sodium light soy sauce

1 tablespoon Chinkiang black rice vinegar or balsamic vinegar

2 pinches of soft brown sugar

2 tablespoons toasted sesame oil

2 tablespoons chilli oil

For the garnish

150g beansprouts

pinch of ground toasted Sichuan pepper

3 spring onions, sliced into julienne strips

1 large handful of coriander

3 tablespoons toasted white sesame seeds

A delicious cold egg noodle salad where the dressing is wokked up and then assembled. The spicy Sichuan flavours are particularly refreshing on a hot summer's day. It can easily be doubled up for a family buffet too! For vegans, substitute the egg noodles with plain wheat flour noodles of your choice.

Serves 4 kcal 521 carbs 58.7g protein 13.9g fat 27.2g

Cook the noodles according to the packet instructions, then drain and refresh under cold running water. Drain well and season with the toasted sesame oil.

Blanch the beansprouts for the garnish in hot water for 10 seconds, then drain and rinse in cold water. Set aside.

Heat a wok over a high heat and add the rapeseed oil, give the oil a swirl, then add the garlic, ginger and chilli and cook, stirring, for a few seconds. Add the chilli bean paste, rice wine or dry sherry, sesame paste or tahini, vegetable stock, tamari or light soy sauce, vinegar, sugar and sesame and chilli oils. Stir well until well combined. Take the wok off the heat and pour in the noodles, tossing them well. Transfer to a serving plate.

Chill in the fridge for 20 minutes, then sprinkle over the Sichuan pepper and serve garnished with the beansprouts, spring onion, toasted sesame seeds and coriander.

8 mins

4 mins

Ve GF DF

WOK FRIED GINGER MISO SPINACH

1 tablespoon peanut oil

1 pinch of salt

2 garlic cloves, peeled and crushed, left whole

400g baby spinach leaves

For the ginger miso sauce

2.5cm piece of fresh ginger, peeled and grated

1 tablespoon organic red miso paste

1 tablespoon tamari or low-sodium light soy sauce

50ml hot water

1 tablespoon Shaohsing rice wine or dry sherry

pinch of caster sugar

For the garnish

1–2 spring onions, topped and tailed, finely sliced

2 teaspoons toasted sesame seeds

A simple vegan stir fry of baby spinach leaves that are wilted and seasoned in a gingery miso sauce, making a deliciously moreish light supper served with rice.

Serves 2 kcal 122 carbs 3.6g protein 13.9g fat 27.2g

In a jug, whisk together the ingredients for the sauce and stir until well combined.

Heat a wok over a high heat and add the peanut oil. Give it a swirl, and then add the salt to dissolve, then the garlic and stir for a few seconds, then add the spinach. Cook, tossing the spinach for a few seconds and then add the sauce and toss with the spinach. Cook the spinach down in the sauce to wilt it.

To serve, spoon some of the ginger miso spinach over jasmine rice, garnish with the spring onions and toasted sesame seeds and eat immediately.

30 mins

+ 3½ hours dough proving time

15 mins

Ve DF

MOCK DUCK BLACK PEPPER WITH BASIL SHEN JIAN BAO (STEAMED BUNS)

300g plain flour

30g caster sugar

¼ teaspoon salt

1 teaspoon fast-action dried yeast

2 tablespoons rapeseed oil

2.5cm piece of fresh ginger, peeled and grated

15g dried shiitake mushrooms, soaked in hot water for 20 minutes, drained and finely diced

½ tablespoon cornflour, blended with 2 tablespoons cold water

150g Chinese leaf, finely chopped

½ tablespoon sesame oil

90g mock duck, finely chopped

2 spring onions, finely chopped

pinch of cracked black pepper

2 tablespoons vegetarian oyster sauce

5g basil leaves, finely shredded

For the seasoning sauce

¼ teaspoon salt

½ vegetable stock cube, grated

¼ teaspoon caster sugar

¼ teaspoon ground white pepper

1 tablespoon tamari or low-sodium light soy sauce

contd overleaf

Although this isn't the quickest recipe in this book, it's worth the effort as it's super delicious, especially if you like a fluffy bao with a savoury peppery filling. I've gone all vegan on this one, but you can use cooked meats if you prefer. The trick to achieving a golden pan-fried bottom and a moist soft top is to make sure your wok or saucepan has an even, flat bottom and a tight-fitting lid with a hole that allows the steam to escape. Eat while they're still piping hot, and dunk them into some thick sweet soy sauce.

Makes 18 buns kcal 97 carbs 18.3g protein 2.6g fat 2g*

In a large bowl, mix the flour, sugar, salt and yeast with 180ml lukewarm water. Knead the mixture for 10–12 minutes until elastic. Cover with a clean tea towel and leave in a warm place for 3 hours to prove until it has doubled in size.

Punch the air out and divide the dough into 18 small balls of 20–25g each. Knead the balls individually, then cover and leave in a warm place to prove for a further 20 minutes.

Combine all the ingredients for the seasoning sauce.

Heat a wok over a medium heat, 1 tablespoon of the rapeseed oil and give the oil a swirl. Fry the ginger for 30 seconds. Add the mushrooms and seasoning sauce and stir-fry for 1 minute. Stir in the blended cornflour and stir-fry for 1 minute or until the sauce thickens. Add the Chinese leaf and sesame oil and fry briefly to make sure all the ingredients are thoroughly mixed. Remove from the heat.

Add the mock duck, and spring onions into the Chinese leaf mixture and mix well. Season further with the black pepper and vegetarian oyster sauce and toss in the shredded basil leaves.

To serve
small dish of thick soy sauce
small dish of sweet chilli sauce
small dish of equal amounts of
    vegetarian oyster sauce and
    sriracha chilli sauce, mixed

*per bao

Flatten the dough balls. Using a rolling pin, roll over each flattened dough a few times. Then, taking the dough by the edge, gently go over the edge of the dough with the rolling pin. The aim is to try and achieve a round dough sheet of a thickness of around 3mm in the middle with a much thinner edge of around 1mm.

Taking a dough sheet in the palm of your hand, place a generous tablespoonful of the vegetable mixture in the middle. Then cup your palm so the filling remains in the middle of the dough sheet; gently gather the edge of the sheet into the middle and twist to seal the edge. It's a bit like making a Xiao long bao, except this time, the filling is concealed within the dough.

Continue until all the dough sheets are filled. Heat a wok over a low heat, add the remaining rapeseed oil and give the oil a swirl. Arrange the filled dough buns around the pan (cook in two batches, depending on the size of your wok), leaving a 5mm space in between so the dough buns have enough space to rise during cooking. Cover and cook for 1–2 minutes, then add water to cover half of the filled buns and sprinkle some water over the top of the buns.

Turn the heat to medium, cover with a lid and cook until all the water has evaporated and the bottom of the buns has turned crispy and golden brown. Serve with a small dish each of thick soy sauce, sweet chilli sauce and vegetarian oyster mixed with sriracha chilli sauce.

5 mins

2 mins

Ve GF DF

GARLIC WOK TOSSED BABY PAK CHOY

1 tablespoon rapeseed oil
1 pinch of sea salt
2 garlic cloves, peeled, crushed finely chopped
200g baby pak choy, washed, sliced in half down the length
1 tablespoon Shaohsing rice wine or dry sherry
1 teaspoon toasted sesame oil

One of my favourite ways of serving pak choy, this is a deliciously crunchy side that is also incredibly quick and easy to make.

Serves 4 kcal 87 carbs 3.1g protein 1.7g fat 7.2g

Heat a wok over high heat, add the rapeseed oil, give the oil a swirl and then add the sea salt and finely chopped garlic. Add the baby pak choy, toss wokking to 30 seconds. Add the shaohsing rice wine or dry sherry and cook for another 30 seconds until the leaves have wilted but still aldente.

Season with sesame oil. Remove and serve.

20 mins

to cook the sushi rice
+ 20 minutes chill time
for the rice

5–6
mins

Ve GF DF

For the rice
250g short-grain sushi rice,
    washed well and drained
½ teaspoon vegetable bouillon
    powder

For the vegetables
1 tablespoon peanut oil
½ tablespoon finely chopped
    garlic
1 teaspoon deseeded and finely
    chopped red chilli
1 tablespoon finely chopped
    shallots
100g fresh sweetcorn, kernels
    removed
90g baby asparagus, sliced into
    1cm rounds
70g fresh shiitake mushrooms,
    stalks removed, diced
3 tablespoons tamari or low-
    sodium light soy sauce
1 tablespoon Shaohsing rice wine
    or dry sherry
1 teaspoon toasted sesame oil
2 pinches of ground white
    pepper

To serve (optional)
2 large eggs
1 tablespoon peanut oil

For the garnish
4 x 7cm x 4cm pieces of roasted
    seaweed, torn into 2.5cm
    pieces
½ teaspoon Japanese togarashi
    dried chilli peppers

VEGGIE SEAWEED ASPARAGUS FRIED RICE WITH OPTIONAL FRIED EGGS

The sweetcorn, asparagus and roasted seaweed add a delicious sweet and umami flavour to this dish, and sushi rice, as an alternative to the usual jasmine rice, gives a slightly sticky and satisfying starchiness (in a good way). Non-vegans can top with two fried runny eggs, if they like.

Serves 2 kcal 719 carbs 116.2g protein 22.3g fat 21.4g

Place the drained rice in a medium pan, stir in the vegetable bouillon powder and 450ml water and bring to the boil. Turn the heat to low, cover the pan and cook for 15 minutes. Remove the lid, fluff up the rice and spread out on a tray, then leave to cool at room temperature for 15–20 minutes.

Heat a wok over a high heat until smoking, add the peanut oil and give it a swirl. Add the garlic, chilli and shallots and stir for a few seconds to release their aroma. Add the sweetcorn and wok-fry for 10 seconds, then add the asparagus and wok-fry for a further few seconds. Add the mushrooms and cook for 1 minute. Season with 1 tablespoon of the tamari and the rice wine or dry sherry.

Push the vegetables to the side of the wok, add the rice and toss, cooking until all the ingredients are well combined. Season with the remaining tamari, the sesame oil and white pepper.

Remove the fried rice and place in two clay pots. Put the lids on and keep the rice warm in a low oven while you cook the eggs, if you're serving these.

When ready to serve, if you like, fry the eggs in the peanut oil, sunny-side up, until crispy on the bottom. Top each portion of rice with an egg and sprinkle each with half the seaweed and togarashi chilli pepper.

FISH &

SHELLFISH

5 mins

5-8 mins

GF DF

TAIWANESE-STYLE SEAFOOD 'PANCAKE'

40g potato flour

40g cornflour

2 spring onions, finely diced

1 red chilli, deseeded and finely diced

2 tablespoons rapeseed oil

100g fresh mixed seafood (squid rings, mussels and tiger prawns)

2 eggs

75g pak choy, each leaf sliced down the stalk into 5mm strips

sliced spring onions, to garnish

For the sweet hot sauce

2 tablespoons hoisin sauce

2 tablespoons oyster sauce

2 teaspoons sriracha chilli sauce

This delicious snack or quick mid-week supper is inspired by my love of the oyster omelettes that you get in the street food stalls found in the night markets in Taiwan. It involves making a thin, egg crêpe-like pancake. The trick is to stir-fry the seafood first and then pour in the potato and cornflour batter and cook it like a thin eggy crêpe. Serve it with a spicy sweet concoction of hoisin, oyster and sriracha sauces – so umami and full of yum!

If you're vegan, you can use an assortment of sliced fresh shiitake, shimeji and enoki mushrooms instead of the seafood.

Serves 2 kcal 415 carbs 48g protein 17.6g fat 17.4g

Combine all the ingredients for the sweet hot sauce and set aside.

Mix the potato flour and cornflour in 80ml cold water, then add the diced spring onions and chilli.

Heat a wok over a medium heat, add 1 tablespoon of the rapeseed oil and give the oil a swirl. Add half the mixed seafood and fry for a few seconds, then add half the spring onion and chilli mixture. Lightly beat one of the eggs and add to the wok with half the pak choy.

Cook for 2–3 minutes until the potato starch has turned a translucent colour. Spoon out onto a serving plate and cover with foil to keep it warm. Make the second 'pancake' in the same way, using the remaining ingredients.

To serve, drizzle with the sweet hot sauce and garnish with some sliced spring onions.

20 mins

5 mins

DF

OYSTER SAUCE, MISO AND HONEY SPICED PRAWN CHOW MEIN

For the marinade

1 tablespoon freshly grated
   peeled ginger

1 tablespoon organic miso paste

2 tablespoons oyster sauce

1 teaspoon dark soy sauce

1 tablespoon plain flour

For the stir-fry

12 large raw tiger prawns, tails on,
   shelled and deveined

2 tablespoons rapeseed oil

1 garlic clove, peeled and
   crushed

1 red chilli deseeded and finely
   chopped

1 tablespoon Shaohsing rice wine
   or dry sherry

2 tablespoons runny honey

2 tablespoons tamari or low-
   sodium light soy sauce

1 teaspoon chilli oil

350g cooked egg noodles,
   seasoned with toasted
   sesame oil

For the garnish

large handful of beansprouts

2 spring onions, sliced into rings
   on the diagonal (optional)

An all-round Asian fusion dish that is salty, spicy and sweet. The miso, oyster sauce and honey work particularly well with the sweetness of the prawns. It's perfect with cooked egg noodles tossed through.

Serves 2 kcal 534 carbs 83.4g protein 21.2g fat 15.2g

Combine all the ingredients for the marinade in a bowl and mix well to form a paste. Add the prawns, toss to coat and leave to marinate for 15 minutes.

Heat a wok over a high heat and add the rapeseed oil. Give the oil a swirl, then add the garlic and chilli and cook, stirring, for a few seconds to release their aroma. Add the marinated prawns and cook tossing for 1 minute. Season with the rice wine, honey, tamari or light soy sauce and chilli oil, and coat well. Continue to cook, tossing, to caramelise the prawns for another minute until they have turned pink. Add the noodles and toss through to mix well.

Serve immediately garnished with the beansprouts and spring onion slices.

15 mins

10 mins

GF DF

CRISPY 'FAMILY SNAPPER' WITH BLACK BEAN SAUCE

For the black bean sauce
50g fermented salted black
    beans
1 tablespoon Shaohsing rice wine
    or dry sherry
1 tablespoon peanut oil
2 tablespoons grated garlic
2 tablespoons freshly grated
    peeled ginger
1 red chilli, deseeded and finely
    chopped
250ml chicken or vegetable stock
1 teaspoon tamari or low-sodium
    light soy sauce
pinch of ground white pepper, or
    to taste
1 tablespoon cornflour, blended
    with 2 tablespoons cold water

For the snapper
1 x 500g whole red snapper,
    cleaned and scaled
100g potato flour
coarse salt, to taste
1–2 teaspoons ground white
    pepper, or to taste
vegetable oil, for deep-frying

For the garnish
edible flowers
1–2 spring onions, cut into
    julienne strips

Perfect for a Chinese New Year Party, this spectacular dish is very easy to make. If you prefer, you could use chunks of cod and serve it in a fish-shaped platter – the skeleton is really just for an 'X-factor' presentation. Serve with jasmine rice and steamed greens.

Serves 4 kcal 220 carbs 25.8g protein 17.6g fat 5.3g

To make the sauce, soak the beans in cold water for a few minutes to remove the salt. Drain and pour over the rice wine or dry sherry then use a fork or the back of a spoon to mash them up.

Heat a wok over a high heat until smoking, add the oil and give it a swirl. Add the garlic, ginger and chilli and stir-fry briefly until just beginning to brown and catch on the wok. Add the beans, stir briefly, and then add the stock, tamari or light soy sauce and white pepper. Bring to the boil, stirring, add the blended cornflour and cook until the sauce thickens and is glistening.

Fillet the fish, keeping the skeleton whole with the head intact. Cut the fish into 5cm cubes. Mix together the potato flour, salt and white pepper and lightly dust the skeleton and head. Toss the fish pieces in the flour mixture until well coated, then shake off the excess.

Heat about 7.5cm of oil in the deep-fryer or a wok to 180°C. Using two metal skewers, pierce the fish skeleton in two spots to secure it in a slightly curved shape. Gently lower the skeleton into the oil and fry briefly on both sides until light golden. Drain on kitchen paper and set aside. When ready to serve, deep-fry the fish quickly until cooked through and just beginning to turn light golden, about 1–2 minutes.

Arrange the fish skeleton, standing upright, on a serving platter and pile the fish pieces either side. You can pour the hot black bean sauce over the fish and place the rest in a gravy boat for guests to pour over rice. Garnish with edible flowers and the spring onion strips and serve.

PRAWN 'BAN' MEIN

10 mins

6 mins

DF

For the noodles

250g dried wheat flour noodles
1 tablespoon toasted sesame oil

For the stir-fry

2 tablespoons peanut oil
½ teaspoon ground toasted
    Sichuan peppercorns
2 red chillies, deseeded and
    finely chopped
2 spring onions, finely chopped
250g raw tiger prawns, shelled
    with heads off, tails on,
    deveined
100g beansprouts
small handful of coriander

For the sauce

100ml cold vegetable stock
2 tablespoons tamari or low-
    sodium light soy sauce
1 tablespoon toasted sesame oil
1 tablespoon Chinkiang black
    rice vinegar or balsamic
    vinegar
1 teaspoon chilli oil
1 tablespoon cornflour

Both a 'ban' mein and a 'chow' mein contains stir-fried prawns, but a 'ban' mein is saucy rather than dry stir-fry. This woks in less than 6 minutes and makes great use of your store cupboard ingredients. I've used beansprouts for their satisfying crunch, but you could use any seasonal vegetables of your choice. It's such a versatile dish, you'll make it time and time again.

Serves 2 kcal 825 carbs 102.9g protein 40.3g fat 27g

Put all the sauce ingredients in a jug and mix well.

Cook the noodles according to packet instructions and drain well. Drizzle with the sesame oil to prevent them from sticking together.

Heat a wok over a high heat until smoking, add the peanut oil and give the oil a swirl. Add the ground Sichuan peppercorns, red chillies and spring onions and toss for a few seconds. Add the prawns and cook for 1 minute. Pour in the sauce and bring to the boil, then add the cooked noodles and toss together well to coat in the sauce until the prawns are pink. Add the beansprouts and give it all one last toss, then sprinkle the coriander on top and serve immediately.

YU SIANG HALIBUT

15 mins

10 mins

GF DF

400g whole halibut fillets, skinned
pinch of salt
pinch of ground white pepper
1 tablespoon Shaohsing rice wine
    or dry sherry
1 teaspoon cornflour, blended
    with 1 tablespoon cold water
2 tablespoons rapeseed oil
2 garlic cloves, finely chopped
2.5cm piece of fresh ginger, finely
    peeled and grated
1 red chilli, deseeded and finely
    chopped
1 spring onion, finely sliced

For the sauce

1 tablespoon chilli bean paste
100ml cold vegetable stock
1 tablespoon tamari or low-
    sodium light soy sauce
1 tablespoon Chinkiang black
    rice vinegar or balsamic
    vinegar
1 tablespoon cornflour

For the garnish

1 spring onion, sliced into strips
    and soaked in iced water for
    5 minutes to curl, then drained
coriander leaves

When I was working with Ken Hom on the television series *Exploring China*, we filmed with famed chef Yu Bo, who made us his spectacular yu siang prawn dish. Yu siang was originally a dish of braised pork and aubergines but translates as 'fish fragrant'. Some Sichuan chefs contend that fish sauce was used in the original sauce, hence the name, but we may never know the answer to this conundrum. In any case, I'm making it here with meaty halibut. It's quick, easy and delicious, and for once 'yu siang' sauce is actually appropriate!

Serves 2 kcal 366 carbs 17.2g protein 41g fat 15g

Place the fish fillets on a deep, heatproof serving plate. Season with the salt, white pepper, rice wine or dry sherry and the blended cornflour.

Set the plate on a steamer set over a wok filled halfway with water. Place the lid on and steam the fish over a medium heat for 8 minutes.

Meanwhile, combine all the ingredients for the sauce in a bowl and mix well.

Heat another wok over a high heat until smoking, add the rapeseed oil and swirl the oil around. Wok-fry the garlic, ginger, chilli and spring onion for a few seconds, then add the sauce and bring to the boil, then set over a very low heat and whisk until the sauce is smooth.

Remove the fish from the steamer to serving plates. Pour the sauce over the fish, garnish with the spring onion curls and coriander leaves and serve immediately with jasmine rice.

10 mins

8 mins

GF DF

STEAMED HADDOCK FILLETS WITH WOK-FRIED BACON

315g haddock fillets, skinned and
    cut into 2.5cm chunks
pinch of salt
pinch of ground white pepper
1 tablespoon cornflour, blended
    with 2 tablespoons cold water
1 tablespoon freshly grated
    peeled ginger
1 spring onion, sliced into strips
    and soaked in iced water for 5
    minutes to curl, then drained,
    to garnish

For the wok-fry
1 tablespoon rapeseed oil
1 teaspoon ground Sichuan
    peppercorns
2 dried red chillies
1 teaspoon freshly grated peeled
    ginger
150g smoked bacon lardons,
    diced
½ teaspoon ground turmeric
1 tablespoon Shaohsing rice
    wine or dry sherry
1 teaspoon dark soy sauce
1 tablespoon tamari or low-
    sodium light soy sauce
juice of ½ lemon or 1 tablespoon
    Chinkiang black rice vinegar
    or balsamic vinegar
2 teaspoons chilli oil

**I have become a huge fan of wok-steaming fish for a quick,
healthy supper. Haddock fillets have a firm, flaking texture
when cooked and are delish with wokked-up spicy bacon
lardons on top. Perfect served with some blanched or
steamed greens and jasmine rice.**

Serves 2 kcal 445 carbs 13.7g protein 41.9g fat 25.6g

Place the haddock on a heatproof serving plate and season
with the salt, white pepper and blended cornflour, then cover
with the grated ginger.

Set the plate on a steamer rack set over a wok filled halfway
with water. Place the lid on and steam the haddock over a
medium-high heat for 6 minutes.

Meanwhile, heat another wok over a high heat until smoking,
add the rapeseed oil and give it a swirl. Add the Sichuan
peppercorns, dried chillies and ginger and stir for a few seconds
to release their aroma. Add the lardons and turmeric and
wok-fry for a few seconds, then season with the rice wine or dry
sherry, the dark soy sauce, tamari or light soy sauce, lemon juice
or vinegar and the chilli oil.

Remove the fish from the steamer to serving plates. Spoon the
wok-fried lardons on top, then garnish with the spring onion
curls. Set on the table with some blanched or steamed greens
and serve with jasmine rice.

THAI COCONUT COD CURRY

500g cod loins, skinned, deboned, sliced into 2.5cm chunks
pinch of salt
pinch of ground white pepper
2 tablespoons Thai red curry paste, plus 1 teaspoon
1 tablespoon cornflour, blended with 2 tablespoons cold water
2 tablespoons rapeseed oil
2 baby shallots, sliced, or ½ white onion, diced
1 stalk of lemongrass, any tough outer leaf discarded, sliced on the angle into 4cm lengths
200ml coconut milk
100ml vegetable stock
1 tablespoon fish sauce
100g sugarsnap peas or mangetout

For the garnish
Thai basil leaves
1 red chilli, sliced, seeds in

When I need a warming curry, I instinctively go for this super delicious, quick and easy wok dish that can be on the table in less than 20 minutes. All you have to do is arm yourself with some cod, shallots, sugarsnap peas and red chillies and some store cupboard staples like coconut milk, fish sauce and Thai red curry paste, and the rest is easy.

If you're vegan, substitute fried tofu chunks and oyster mushrooms for the cod, and vegetarian oyster sauce for the fish sauce.

Serves 2 kcal 406 carbs 20.4g protein 47.6g fat 13.4g

Season the cod with salt and ground white pepper. Using a brush, brush 1 teaspoon of the Thai red curry paste onto the fish, then pour the blended cornflour over the fish.

Heat a wok over a medium heat, add 1 tablespoon of the rapeseed oil and give the oil a swirl. Add the shallots or onion and lemongrass and stir-fry for a few seconds to release their aroma.

Add the 2 tablespoons of Thai red curry paste and stir around to distribute in the wok. Add the remaining rapeseed oil and the marinated cod and sear the fish for a few seconds. Pour in a little water around the edges of the wok to help create some steam, then add the coconut milk and stock. Bring to the boil and gently poach the cod for about 5 minutes until it has turned opaque white.

Season with the fish sauce, then add the sugarsnap peas or mangetout and cook for 30 seconds. Spoon out, garnish with the Thai basil and sliced red chilli and serve with jasmine rice.

20 mins

+ 15 minutes to cook the rice

3 mins

DF

KIRAKUYA FIREBALLS

115g fresh tuna or salmon, or
  sushi-grade smoked salmon,
  diced
3 tablespoons mayonnaise
2 tablespoons sake
1 teaspoon sriracha chilli sauce
1 teaspoon finely sliced
  coriander stems
125g cooked sushi rice
1 tablespoon seasoned sushi rice
  vinegar
1 teaspoon caster sugar
1 large egg, beaten
125g panko breadcrumbs
vegetable oil, for deep-frying

For the sake-soy dipping sauce
6 tablespoons sake
4 tablespoons tamari or low-
  sodium light soy sauce
juice of ½ lemon
1 tablespoon caster sugar

For the wasabi mayonnaise
4 tablespoons mayonnaise
4 teaspoons wasabi paste

*per fireball

This memorable dish is one I created for Kirakuya, a Japanese sake bar in midtown Manhattan, when I was filming *Restaurant Redemption* back in 2014. It went down a storm. I called them fireballs because they are full of flavour and heat! They consists of hot fish encased in sushi rice and covered in panko breadcrumbs. Deep-fried until golden, they're served with a boozy sake-soy dipping sauce and/or wasabi mayonnaise.

Makes 8 kcal 160 carbs 15g protein 6.7g fat 8.1g*

Combine all the ingredients for the sake-soy dipping sauce in a small bowl and stir until the sugar is dissolved.

Combine the mayonnaise and wasabi paste in another small bowl.

In a mixing bowl, combine the diced tuna, salmon or smoked salmon, the mayonnaise, sake, sriracha chilli sauce and coriander stems.

Lay the cooked sushi rice flat out on a baking tray. In a small bowl, mix the seasoned rice vinegar with the sugar until dissolved, then drizzle over the cooked sushi rice.

Using a small scoop or measuring spoon, scoop a 2 tablespoon-portion of rice and form into a rough ball. Press a hole into the centre of the rice ball and stuff with 1 tablespoon of the fish mixture. Press the opening closed and roll the ball between your hands to reform. Repeat until all the fish mixture and rice are used.

Place the beaten egg in a small bowl and the panko breadcrumbs in a shallow dish or on a pie plate.

Roll the fish rice balls in the beaten egg and then into the breadcrumbs to coat.

Add enough oil to a wok for deep-frying and heat to 180°C. Deep-fry the rice balls for 2–3 minutes until golden brown. Drain on kitchen paper. Serve immediately with the sake-soy dipping sauce and wasabi mayonnaise.

15 mins

10 mins

GF DF

CHING'S FISH BALL NOODLE SOUP

Ever since I tried my first steaming bowl of fish ball noodle soup in Hong Kong, I have been obsessed with it. The balls have a delicious 'chew' to them – spongy in a fishy, delicate way – and they're served in a moreish, oniony broth, with clear rice noodles and umami seaweed. I like the soup ladened with lashings of a lip-smackingly hot chilli oil – you get my point.

This is my version and it doesn't disappoint; the trick is to add squid, which hardens when cooked and gives the fish more of a satisfying 'chew'. I reckon my homemade fishballs are even better than some manufactured ones, which contain too much starch and not enough fish. I hope you enjoy them.

Serves 2   kcal 327   carbs 36.2g   protein 29.2g   fat 8.4g

For the fish balls
200g whole haddock fillets, skinned and finely chopped
50g squid, cleaned and minced
pinch of salt flakes
pinch of ground white pepper
1 teaspoon Shaohsing rice wine or dry sherry
1 tablespoon cornflour
1 large egg white
1 teaspoon oyster sauce
1 tablespoon finely sliced coriander stems

For the broth
1.5 litres fresh fish stock
200g Chinese leaf, cut into 2.5cm slices
200g cooked vermicelli rice noodles
pinch of salt flakes
pinch of ground white pepper
1 tablespoon tamari or low-sodium light soy sauce
1 teaspoon toasted sesame oil

To serve
1 teaspoon chilli oil, or to taste
fresh coriander leaves
1 tablespoon chopped chives

Place the haddock and squid in a food processor, season with the salt, white pepper, rice wine or dry sherry, the cornflour, egg white and oyster sauce and blend well until airy and light. Sprinkle in the coriander stems and mix well. Using 2 tablespoons, pass some of the mixture from spoon to spoon, turning the mixture until an oval ball (quenelle) is formed – you should get 12 balls.

Add the fish stock to a large wok and bring to a simmer. Add the Chinese leaf and cook for 1 minute. Add the cooked noodles and season with the salt and white pepper.

Turn the heat to medium and gently add the fish balls to the wok. Cook for 2–3 minutes until the fish balls float to the surface and turn opaque white.

Season with the tamari or light soy sauce and sesame oil.

Divide the noodles between two bowls, ladle in the stock and Chinese leaves and place six fish balls into each bowl. Drizzle with the chilli oil, sprinkle over the coriander leaves and chives and serve immediately.

20 mins

4 mins

GF DF

BANG BANG CHILLI BEAN PRAWN NOODLE SALAD

For the prawns

1 tablespoon rapeseed oil

10 large raw tiger prawns, shelled and deveined

1 teaspoon chilli bean paste

1 teaspoon Chinkiang black rice vinegar or balsamic vinegar

1 teaspoon tamari or low-sodium light soy sauce

For the noodles

100g dried vermicelli mung bean noodles, soaked in hot water for 5–6 minutes, drained

½ cucumber, deseeded and sliced into long julienne strips

40g radishes, thinly sliced

40g carrots, sliced into long julienne strips

1 red chilli, deseeded and finely chopped

1 large spring onion, finely sliced

toasted mixed black and white sesame seeds, to sprinkle

For the dressing

2 tablespoons rapeseed oil

1 tablespoon grated ginger

1 tablespoon toasted sesame oil

2 tablespoons sesame paste

1 tablespoon crunchy peanut butter

1 tablespoon tamari or low-sodium light soy sauce

2 tablespoons black rice vinegar

½ teaspoon dried chilli flakes

½ teaspoon ground Sichuan peppercorns

This is my take on the Sichuan bang bang chicken noodle salad. Quick and easy, it's low in calories too! The prawns are wok-fried in chilli bean paste, black rice vinegar and soy, then served whilst they are still hot on the cold noodle salad. I love the bit of ying and yang that this dish brings.

If you are vegan, use shimeji mushrooms instead of the prawns.

Serves 2 kcal 611 carbs 52.3g protein 14.6g fat 38.8g

Place all the dressing ingredients in a bowl and whisk well to combine to a smooth dressing.

Arrange the drained noodles on two serving plates. Layer the cucumber, radishes, carrots, red chilli and spring onion on top. Cover with clingfilm and chill in the fridge until ready to serve.

Heat a wok over a high heat until smoking, add the rapeseed oil and give the oil a swirl. Add the tiger prawns, chilli bean paste, vinegar and tamari or light soy sauce and toss for 1 minute or until the prawns have all turned pink and are cooked through.

To serve, remove the noodle salad from the fridge, place the hot spiced prawns on top and sprinkle with some toasted sesame seeds. Spoon some of the dressing over and serve immediately, with the remaining dressing on the side.

GOLDEN MACANESE COD

750g cod loins, cut into 2.5cm
   chunks
pinch of salt
pinch of ground white pepper
1 tablespoon cornflour, blended
   with 2 tablespoons cold water
2 tablespoons rapeseed oil
2 garlic cloves, finely chopped
2 shallots, finely chopped
½ teaspoon ground turmeric
1 teaspoon shrimp paste
500ml vegetable stock
100ml coconut milk
1 tablespoon tamari or low-
   sodium light soy sauce
   (optional)

For the garnish
Thai basil
finely sliced deseeded red
   chillies

For the seasonal salad (optional)
200g baby spinach leaves
100g mangetout
100g baby cherry tomatoes
1 medium red onion, diced
1 tablespoon extra-virgin olive oil
juice of 1 lemon
pinch of salt
pinch of cracked black pepper

This dish is inspired by Macanese golden cod, but I'm using fresh cod instead of dried (bacalhau) and I also add vegetable stock and shrimp paste to give more sauce, as well as a deeper savoury umami flavour. Serve with jasmine rice and a large seasonal salad.

If you are vegan, use plain firm tofu instead of the cod, and a vegetable bouillon stock cube instead of the shrimp paste.

Serves 4 kcal 304 carbs 16.4g protein 37.3g fat 10.6g

Place the cod in a bowl and season with the salt and white pepper. Add the blended cornflour and toss the fish to coat well, then set aside.

Heat a wok over a medium heat, add 1 tablespoon of the rapeseed oil and give it a swirl. Add the garlic and shallots and fry for about 30 seconds until translucent and caramelised at the edges. Add the turmeric and shrimp paste and stir for a few seconds, then add the remaining rapeseed oil and quickly add the cod. Sear the fish on one side and then, using a spatula, gently turn the pieces to sear on the other side. Pour in the vegetable stock and coconut milk and bring to the boil, then cook over a medium heat for about 4 minutes, until the liquid turns a deeper yellow in colour and the cod turns an opaque white and is cooked. Season further to taste with the tamari or light soy sauce, if you like.

Garnish with Thai basil and sliced red chillies and serve immediately with a seasonal salad (simply toss all the salad ingredients together), if you like, and jasmine rice.

30-40 mins

12 mins

DF

MACANESE-STYLE CODFISH AND POTATO BALLS

375g cod loins, cut into 2.5cm chunks
500g baby potatoes, scrubbed
1 tablespoon rapeseed oil
2 garlic cloves, finely chopped
1 shallot, finely chopped
½ teaspoon ground turmeric
1 teaspoon shrimp paste
100ml coconut milk
30ml vegetable stock
200ml peanut or vegetable oil, for deep-frying

For the marinade
pinch of sea salt
pinch of ground white pepper
1 tablespoon cornflour blended with 2 tablespoons cold water

For the seasoning mix
1 stalk of lemongrass, grated
½ red cayenne chilli, deseeded and finely diced
2 spring onions, finely diced
5 sprigs of coriander, leaves and stems finely chopped
2 pinches of salt
2 pinches of ground white pepper

For the coating
100g plain flour
5 eggs, lightly beaten
200g panko breadcrumbs

*per fish and potato ball

These are my take on Macanese fish and potato balls. The beauty of the dish is that you can make them in advance, freeze them and then bake from frozen. Perfect served with a zesty red cabbage and tomato salad with a lemon, soy, olive oil, salt and black pepper dressing.

Makes 12 kcal 225 carbs 26.4g protein 11.9g fat 8.4g*

Combine all the ingredients for the marinade in a bowl and mix well to form a paste. Add the cod and toss to coat.

Bring 1.5 litres water to the boil in a medium pan. Add the potatoes and cook for 20 minutes. Drain and, using a fork, mash.

Heat a wok over a medium heat, add the rapeseed oil and swirl in the pan. Add the garlic and shallot and fry for about 30 seconds until translucent and caramelised at the edges. Add the turmeric, shrimp paste and cod. Sear the cod on one side and then, using a spatula, gently turn the pieces and sear on the other side. Pour in the coconut milk and stock, bring to the boil, then cook until the liquid turns a deeper yellow in colour. Remove the cod from the wok and flake using a fork.

Combine the ingredients for the seasoning mix. Add to the mashed potatoes, flaked fish and half of the poaching liquid from the wok, being careful not to break up the fish pieces too much as you want some texture.

Place the flour, eggs and breadcrumbs in three separate bowls. Take 2 large tablespoons of the filling, shape into a ball with a diameter of about 4cm, dip into the flour, then the egg, and then the breadcrumbs to coat. Double coat by repeating the process, and then continue until you have 12 balls.

Heat the peanut or vegetable oil in another wok to 180°C or until a piece of bread turns golden in 15 seconds and floats to the surface. Lower each ball into the oil, one at a time, then, using a ladle, spoon the hot oil over to coat the ball. Fry for about 1 minute until golden and crisp all over. Remove and place on a plate lined with kitchen paper. Serve with a fresh seasonal salad.

10 mins

3 mins

GF DF

SMOKIN' HOT SCALLOPS AND CHINESE CHIVES

2 tablespoons rapeseed oil

1 tablespoon freshly grated peeled ginger

1 small fresh habañero chilli, deseeded and minced

2 small dried red chillies, finely chopped

8 large sea scallops, cleaned

bunch of Chinese chives, sliced into 2.5cm pieces

1 tablespoon Shaohsing wine or vegetable stock

1 tablespoon tamari or light soy sauce

1 tablespoon Chinkiang black rice vinegar or balsamic vinegar

1 teaspoon soft brown sugar

dash of toasted sesame oil

I am a sucker for the sweetness of scallops and the heat of chillies, and when you pair them with aromatic and pungent Chinese chives, you have a match made in culinary heaven. Delicious with jasmine rice and a glass of dry white wine.

Serves 2 kcal 200 carbs 8.4g protein 12.3g fat 13.3g

Heat a wok over a high heat until smoking, add the rapeseed oil and give the oil a swirl. Add the ginger and the fresh and dried chillies and toss for a few seconds. Add the scallops and cook, tossing continuously, for 15 seconds to 1 minute, depending on the size of the scallops. Add the chives and stir-fry for 1 minute, then season the mixture with the Shaohsing wine or vegetable stock, tamari or light soy sauce, vinegar, sugar and sesame oil. Toss until well combined and hot.

Transfer to serving plates and serve immediately with steamed jasmine rice.

15 mins

5 mins

DF

GOLDEN SESAME PRAWN BALLS

340g raw tiger prawns, shelled and deveined, 200g minced in a food processor, 140g cut into 5mm dice

500ml sunflower or vegetable oil, for deep-frying

For the seasoning mix
2.5cm piece of fresh ginger, peeled and grated
1 large spring onion, finely chopped
1 red chilli, deseeded and finely chopped
1 teaspoon Shaohsing rice wine or dry sherry
1 teaspoon tamari or low-sodium light soy sauce
1 large egg white, beaten
1 teaspoon toasted sesame oil
2 tablespoons cornflour
pinch of cracked salt
pinch of ground black pepper

For the coating
100g plain flour
2 large egg yolks, beaten
100g white sesame seeds

For the garnish and salad
small handful of coriander leaves
small handful of mint leaves
1 red chilli, deseeded and finely chopped
2 heads chicory, leaves separated, dressed with sweet chilli sauce and lime juice (optional)

Prawn toast is a firm favourite with my family, but one year I decided instead to make Golden Sesame Prawn Balls – similar to the toast except without the bread. The results were delicious. The trick is to get a minced but chunky consistency, so there is a bite to them and they hold their shape when fried. Delicious and so simple, they make a fab appetiser served with a chicory leaf salad dressed with sweet chilli sauce and a drizzle of lime juice.

Makes 10–12 kcal 147 carbs 10.4g protein 8.2g fat 8.4g*

Put all the ingredients for the seasoning mix into a medium bowl and stir well with a fork to combine. Add the minced and diced prawns to the bowl and mix well to combine. Roll into 10–12 mini ping-pong-sized balls and transfer to a plate.

Place the flour, egg yolks and sesame seeds in three separate bowls. Dip each prawn ball first into the flour, then in the beaten egg yolks and then into the sesame seeds. Set aside.

Heat the sunflower or vegetable oil in a wok over a medium-high heat to 180°C, or until a bread cube dropped in the oil turns golden brown in 15 seconds and floats to the surface. Using a strainer, lower the prawn balls, one at a time, into the oil and cook, tossing gently, for about 2 minutes until golden brown. Drain on kitchen paper and repeat with the remaining balls.

To serve, place the prawn balls on a serving plate and garnish with a sprinkling of coriander, mint leaves, and chopped red chilli. Or serve as a warm salad, if you like, with chicory leaves dressed with sweet chilli sauce and a drizzle of lime juice. Serve immediately.

*per prawn ball

CHUNKY COD LAKSA

250g dried egg noodles
1 tablespoon rapeseed oil
400ml coconut milk
500ml vegetable or fish stock
juice of 1 lime
1 teaspoon soft brown sugar
1 teaspoon fish sauce
200g cod loins, cut into 2.5cm
   chunks, or raw prawns, shelled
   with tails on, deveined
80g beansprouts
pinch of salt
pinch of ground dried chilli flakes
small handful of coriander leaves

For the laksa paste
1 teaspoon ground coriander
1 teaspoon ground cumin
1 teaspoon ground turmeric
½ onion, chopped
40ml coconut milk
1 tablespoon freshly grated
   peeled ginger or galangal
2 garlic cloves, crushed
15g lemongrass, roughly chopped
1 red cayenne chilli, deseeded
   and roughly chopped
1 tablespoon shrimp paste

Laksa is a Malaysian–Chinese curry noodle broth. The spices used travelled from India and the egg noodles came from southern China. It's easy to make your own laksa paste – just blend all the ingredients in a food processor. Then cook up with coconut milk and stock and add cod, crunchy vegetables, such as beansprouts, and fresh herbs, such as coriander, for a fabulously spicy, moreish meal. Enjoy!

Serves 4 kcal 496 carbs 55.1g protein 19.8g fat 24g

Put all the ingredients for the laksa paste into a blender or food processor and whizz to a smooth paste.

Meanwhile, cook the noodles in a pan of boiling water for about 3 minutes, then drain under cold running water to get rid of starch and help keep the noodles springy.

Heat the rapeseed oil in a wok and cook the laksa paste for 1 minute.

Stir in the coconut milk, stock, lime juice, sugar and fish sauce, then bring the soup to the boil and simmer for 20 minutes.

Add the cod or prawns to the soup and simmer until the fish changes colour (becomes opaque) and is cooked through.

Add the beansprouts, salt and chilli flakes to taste.

Divide the noodles evenly between serving bowls and ladle the soup over. Garnish with coriander leaves and serve immediately.

10 mins

5 mins

GF DF

MY MUM'S SRIRACHA KETCHUP PRAWNS

1 tablespoon rapeseed oil
10 large raw tiger prawns, heads off, deveined, shell and tails on
4 tablespoons tomato ketchup
1 teaspoon sriracha chilli sauce
1 tablespoon tamari or low-sodium light soy sauce
small bunch of chives, finely chopped, to garnish
lime wedges, to serve

This is an update on my mum's ketchup prawns recipe. It sounds so wrong but it's actually so yum. She would sometimes add rice and turn it into a seafood ketchup fried rice. The trick is a good ketchup and to also add a splash of soy sauce to give an umaminess to the dish. I have also added a small dash of sriracha chilli sauce to the dish and with that small but powerful update, the result is a tart, sweet, savoury hot dish. Perfect with jasmine rice and some steamed vegetables. I urge you to wok on and try it!

Serves 2 kcal 124 carbs 6.4g protein 19g fat 23g

Heat a wok over a high heat until smoking, add the rapeseed oil and give it a swirl. Add the tiger prawns and stir-fry until pink. Add the ketchup, sriracha and soy sauces and toss, cooking until the sauce has reduced and caramelised.

Garnish with the chives, squeeze some lime juice over and serve immediately with jasmine rice and steamed greens.

5 mins

3 mins

GF DF

DRUNKEN SCALLOPS WITH SAMPHIRE

200g large scallops, cleaned
pinch of salt
pinch of ground white pepper

For the stir-fry
2 tablespoons groundnut oil
2.5cm piece of fresh ginger,
    peeled and grated
3 tablespoons Shaohsing rice
    wine or dry sherry
100g fresh samphire, washed
    and drained
1 tablespoon tamari or low-
    sodium light soy sauce
1 tablespoon Chinkiang black
    rice vinegar or balsamic
    vinegar
2 tablespoons toasted sesame oil

Anything 'drunken' is sure to be a winner and this one certainly is! It's a rich and sumptuous dish and the perfect marriage really. Salty samphire gives a pop of savoury, while the scallops add a delicious winey sweetness when wokked with the Shaohsing rice wine. In fact, it's the perfect celebratory dish for a Chinese New Year Party. Scallops in Chinese culture symbolise 'coins'.

Serves 2 kcal 320 carbs 6.4g protein 19g fat 23g

Season the scallops with the salt and white pepper.

Heat a wok over a high heat until smoking, add the groundnut oil and give it a swirl. Add the ginger and quickly stir-fry for a few seconds. Add the seasoned scallops and cook for 15 seconds, searing them at the edges, then tossing them in the wok. Add the rice wine or dry sherry (if using gas, you can try to catch the flame by tilting the wok near the flames, but be careful when doing this).

Add the samphire to the wok and stir-fry for 1½ minutes, then season with the tamari or light soy sauce, vinegar and sesame oil. Cook for a further minute until all the scallops have turned opaque and are cooked through and the samphire has turned a translucent green but still has a bite. Transfer to a serving dish and serve with brown or jasmine rice.

TIGER PRAWNS WITH SWEET AND SOUR RED ONION STIR-FRY

1 tablespoon rapeseed oil

2 red onions, sliced into half-moon slices

1 tablespoon Shaohsing rice wine or dry sherry

1 teaspoon soft brown sugar

1 tablespoon Chinkiang black rice vinegar or balsamic vinegar

1 green jalapeño chilli, deseeded and finely chopped

150g large cooked peeled tiger prawns

1 tablespoon tamari or low-sodium light soy sauce

toasted sesame seeds, for sprinkling

Sweet and sour onions make a delicious base for juicy tiger prawns in this recipe. Such a quick and easy stir-fry, it's quicker to wok-up this dish than fold your laundry!

Serves 2 kcal 200 carbs 15.4g protein 15g fat 9g

Heat a wok over a high heat until smoking, add the rapeseed oil and give it a swirl. Add the onions and stir-fry for 2 minutes until they start to turn golden brown at the edges. Then add the rice wine or dry sherry, the brown sugar and vinegar and toss for 1 minute. Add the green chilli pieces and cook for 30 seconds. Finally, add the cooked tiger prawns and toss all the ingredients together. Season with the tamari or light soy sauce, take it off the heat and add a small sprinkle of toasted sesame seeds. Serve immediately with steamed jasmine rice or brown rice.

BOOZY DRUNKEN PRAWNS

5 mins

5 mins

GF DF

1 tablespoon rapeseed oil

2.5cm piece of fresh ginger, peeled and sliced into matchsticks

400g large raw unshelled and deveined freshwater prawns, or baby prawns

3–4 tablespoons Shaohsing rice wine or vodka

1–2 tablespoons tamari or low-sodium light soy sauce

2 pinches of ground white pepper

My grandmother always cooked fresh river prawns in a variety of ways – sometimes just stir-fried with garlic, ginger, chilli and salt, other times with light soy sauce and spring onion. She particularly loved cooking with rice wine – a staple in the Chinese store cupboard. This recipe is my simple creation inspired by her – the ginger adds warmth and aroma, while the rice wine adds a bitter sweetness that complements the natural sweetness of the prawns.

Serves 2 kcal 220 carbs 2.8g protein 35.8g fat 7g

Heat a wok over a high heat until smoking, add the rapeseed oil and give the oil a swirl. Add the ginger and toss quickly in the hot oil for a few seconds. Then add the prawns and stir-fry for 2 minutes. Add the rice wine or vodka and cook for 1 minute. The prawns are cooked when they have all turned a pinky-orange colour. Season with the tamari or light soy sauce and white pepper. Serve immediately with stir-fried vegetables and jasmine rice.

5 mins

5-6 mins

GF DF

HADDOCK, GINGER AND BABY PAK CHOY SOUP

250g haddock loins, cut into 1cm slices

2.5cm piece of fresh ginger, peeled and cut into matchsticks

1 tablespoon Shaohsing rice wine or dry sherry

3 fresh shiitake mushrooms, rinsed and sliced

4 baby pak choy, sliced in half down the middle

1 tablespoon vegetable bouillon powder

dash of toasted sesame oil

pinch of salt

pinch of ground white pepper

small handful of coriander

This is a simple, quick and nourishing supper. It pays to buy fish from sustainable sources. I find fish from Norway and Iceland particularly delicious – not surprising given their clean, clear waters. You will love the delicate flavours of this soup, which is perfect for someone recovering from illness – it's soothing, light and full of goodness.

Serves 2 kcal 150 carbs 5g protein 25g fat 3g

Rinse the fish in cold running water. Pour 800ml water into a wok and bring to the boil. Add the fish and all the ingredients up to and including the bouillon powder. Turn the heat to medium and cook for 5 minutes. Season with the sesame oil, salt and white pepper, then stir in the coriander. Transfer to serving bowls and serve immediately.

CRABMEAT SWEETCORN SOUP

2 ripe tomatoes, each sliced into 6 wedges
2 fresh corn cobs, kernels sliced off
1 tablespoon vegetable bouillon powder
250g fresh white crabmeat, cooked and handpicked, ready to eat (or use canned)
2 tablespoons tamari or low-sodium light soy sauce
generous pinch of ground white pepper
1 tablespoon cornflour, blended with 2 tablespoons cold water
2 large eggs, beaten
large dash of toasted sesame oil

For the garnish
1 spring onion, sliced on the angle
sprinkle of toasted sesame seeds (optional)

This is a staple soup I reach for time and time again. Perfect as a delicious light supper, it's very versatile and you can also posh it up by adding crayfish tails, prawns or even wok-fried scallops or lobster tails.

If you are vegan, substitute the crabmeat for smoked tofu cubes and oyster mushroom pieces, and then follow the rest of the recipe, it will be just as delicious!

Serves 2 kcal 452 carbs 31.1g protein 39.7g fat 19.4g

Pour 1 litre water into a wok and bring to a simmering boil. Add the tomatoes and sweetcorn and cook for 3 minutes to break them down. Keeping the heat on a simmering boil, add the bouillon powder and stir well.

Add the crabmeat, tamari or light soy sauce and white pepper to the soup and stir well. Bring the mixture up to a rolling boil and stir in the blended cornflour. Using a fork, create a whirlpool in the stock and stir in the beaten eggs, creating a web-like pattern. Season with the sesame oil, then pour into two bowls.

Garnish with the spring onion and sesame seeds, if you like, and serve immediately with some chunky French bread or gluten-free bread.

2 mins

4 mins

GF DF

SMOKED SALMON AND EGG FRIED RICE

1 tablespoon rapeseed oil, plus 1 teaspoon

2 large spring onions, finely sliced

3 eggs, lightly beaten

350g cooked and cooled jasmine rice

100g whisky oak-smoked Scottish salmon, torn into large strips

1–2 tablespoons tamari or low-sodium light soy sauce

large pinch of freshly ground black pepper

½ teaspoon toasted sesame oil

1 teaspoon sriracha chilli sauce (optional)

I always cook more rice so I have some left over for this easy and super delicious dish. Just fire up the wok, add oil, fry some spring onion, pour in a few beaten eggs, stir to scramble, then add the rice and toss together well, adding in chunky slices of your favourite smoked salmon, then season with soy sauce, black pepper and a small dash of toasted sesame oil for nuttiness and you're done! For a zingy fiery note, a small drizzle of sriracha or your favourite chilli oil will wrap the whole dish up nicely.

For a vegan version, swap the smoked salmon for smoked tofu strips and sliced fresh shiitake mushrooms, it will be just as delish!

Serves 2 kcal 413 carbs 42.6g protein 25g fat 17g

Heat a wok over a high heat until smoking, add the 1 tablespoon of rapeseed oil and give the oil a swirl. Add the spring onions and stir-fry for a few seconds, then add the beaten eggs and stir-fry for 1 minute to scramble into small moist pieces. Push the eggs to one side.

Add the 1 teaspoon of rapeseed oil and the jasmine rice to the wok and fry together for 1 minute, then add the smoked salmon and toss until all the ingredients are thoroughly combined.

Season with the tamari or light soy sauce, black pepper and sesame oil and toss together well. Serve immediately with some sriracha chilli sauce, if you like.

CHICKEN

& DUCK

BLACK PEPPER DUCK AND KALE WOKKED RICE

For the duck
200g duck breasts, skinned and finely diced
¼ teaspoon cracked black pepper
1 teaspoon Shaohsing rice wine or dry sherry
1 teaspoon dark soy sauce
1 teaspoon cornflour

For the fried rice
2 tablespoons rapeseed oil
100g kale, finely chopped
1 garlic clove, finely chopped
1 tablespoon freshly grated peeled ginger
1 red pepper, deseeded and diced
350g cooked brown rice
50g French beans, finely chopped
2 tablespoons tamari or low-sodium light soy sauce
1 teaspoon toasted sesame oil
pinch of ground black pepper
juice of 1 lemon, to serve

Inspired by my love of Macanese black pepper roast duck, which is served with Cantonese gai lan (Chinese broccoli) and rice, I wanted to have all the flavours of the duck and greens in the rice and so here it is – a simple, quick and delicious duck wokked rice.

Serves 2 kcal 526 carbs 61.3g protein 29.9g fat 19.7g

Season the duck with the cracked black pepper, rice wine or dry sherry and dark soy sauce. Sprinkle over the cornflour and set aside.

Heat a wok over a high heat until smoking, add the rapeseed oil and give the oil a swirl. Stir-fry for 2–3 minutes until well done and slightly crisp. Pour the duck and oil into a heatproof colander set over a heatproof bowl and drain the duck well, reserving the oil.

Reheat the wok and add 1 tablespoon of the drained oil. Add the kale, garlic and ginger and stir-fry for 4–5 seconds. Add the red pepper and stir-fry for 30 seconds.

Add the duck, rice, French beans, soy sauce, sesame oil and black pepper and stir-fry for 10–15 seconds until the rice, duck and vegetables are mixed well with the tamari or light soy sauce and everything is heated through. Dress the rice with a squeeze of fresh lemon juice and serve immediately.

15 mins

18 mins

GF DF

GENERAL TSO'S CHICKEN WINGS

sunflower oil, for deep-frying
500g chicken wings, separated at the joints
pinch of salt
pinch of ground white pepper
2 garlic cloves, smashed
4 dried red chillies, roughly chopped

For the sauce
300ml chicken stock
100ml tomato ketchup
3 tablespoons yellow bean paste or miso paste
3 tablespoons cornflour
2 tablespoons sriracha chilli sauce
1 tablespoon Shaohsing rice wine or dry sherry
2 tablespoons runny honey
2 tablespoons tamari or low-sodium light soy sauce
1½ tablespoons soft brown sugar
1 teaspoon dark soy sauce

For the garnish
toasted white sesame seeds
spring onions, sliced into rounds

Sticky, sweet and spicy, this is an easy-to-make, finger lickin' good crowd-pleaser.

If you are vegan, you can use fried tofu and vegetable stock – just make the sauce, toss in the tofu, wok-fry, then grill until the tofu is sticky. Such a versatile dish. Enjoy!

Serves 4 kcal 701 carbs 81.7g protein 39.9g fat 26.3g

Heat a large wok or deep-fryer over a high heat, then fill to a third of its depth with sunflower oil. Heat the oil to 180°C, or until a bread cube dropped in the oil turns golden brown in 15 seconds and floats to the surface.

Season the chicken wings with the salt and white pepper and deep-fry for 12–15 minutes until golden brown and cooked through. Drain on kitchen paper.

For the sauce, pour all the ingredients into a large jug and whisk to combine.

Heat a wok over a high heat until smoking, add 2–3 tablespoons of sunflower oil and give the oil a swirl. Add the garlic and dried chillies and toss for a few seconds, then add the sauce and cook until slightly reduced and the consistency of gravy. Reserve a cupful of sauce, enough to fill a dipping bowl, then toss in the chicken wings.

Preheat the oven-grill to high. Place the wings on a baking sheet and grill for about 2 minutes until the sauce is bubbling. Remove and transfer to a large serving plate and garnish with toasted sesame seeds and sliced spring onions. Serve with the reserved sauce as a dipping sauce.

30 mins

5 mins

DF

CHICKEN AND CHINESE CELERY BOILED WONTONS IN A SICHUAN-CHINKIANG VINEGAR DRESSING

For the filling
80g dried shiitake mushrooms
450g minced chicken
3 tablespoons finely chopped
    Chinese celery with leaves
1 tablespoon finely grated fresh
    ginger
1 tablespoon tamari or low-
    sodium light soy sauce
1 tablespoon cornflour
1 tablespoon Shaohsing rice wine
    or dry sherry
1 tablespoon chicken bouillon
    powder
1 teaspoon toasted sesame oil
1 teaspoon salt
1 egg white
½ teaspoon ground white pepper

For the wontons
cornflour, for dusting
16 x 7.5cm wonton wrappers

For the vinegar dressing
2 tablespoons tamari or low-
    sodium light soy sauce
2 tablespoons chilli oil
1 tablespoon Chinkiang black
    rice vinegar or balsamic vinegar
½ teaspoon Sichuan
    peppercorns, crushed
1 teaspoon toasted sesame oil

For the garnish
chopped cucumber
coriander leaves

This is one of those healthy Chinese dishes that is low in calories yet feels so satisfying and comforting. The chicken is delicate and the aniseed notes of the celery work so well with the seasoning of white pepper. The wontons are served with a Sichuan pepper and Chinkiang black rice vinegar – fusing Chinese west and Chinese east. I like to make a whole large batch of these and then boil them from frozen for a quick, easy dinner. For a more substantial dinner, serve with some noodles and lashings of chilli oil.

Makes 16 kcal 101 carbs 11.7g protein 8.5g fat 2.6g*

For the filling, soak the shiitake mushrooms in hot water for 10 minutes, then drain, discard the stalks and finely chop. In a bowl, combine them with the chicken, celery, ginger, tamari or light soy sauce, cornflour, rice wine or dry sherry, the chicken bouillon, sesame oil, salt, egg white and white pepper. Mix well and set aside.

For the wontons, line a baking sheet with greaseproof paper and dust lightly with cornflour. Take one wonton wrapper and place 1 teaspoon of the filling in the centre. Gather up the sides and mould around the filling, making a ball shape and twisting the top to secure. Repeat with the remaining wrappers and filling, lining them up on the prepared baking sheet.

Drop the wontons into boiling water in a wok and cook until they float to the surface, about 3–5 minutes.

Combine all the ingredients for the vinegar dressing in a bowl. Stir and set aside.

To serve, divide the wontons between two plates. Surround with the chopped cucumber, drizzle with the vinegar sauce and top with the coriander. Serve immediately.

*per wonton

15 mins

60 mins

GF

MACANESE-STYLE CHICKEN CURRY

2 tablespoons vegetable oil

850g mixed chicken thighs and drumsticks, skinned, bone in, each piece halved across the bone (ask your butcher to prepare this for you)

450g new potatoes, skin on

300g glutinous rice

100g tenderstem broccoli or Chinese gai lan broccoli, cut on the angle into 5cm pieces

salt and ground white pepper, to taste

For the curry

2 tablespoons unsalted butter

1 tablespoon vegetable oil

3 garlic cloves, finely chopped

3 small shallots, diced

2 onions, diced

6 teaspoons Madras curry powder

50g desiccated coconut

140g aubergines, roll cut, then sliced into 5cm finger slices

250ml can coconut milk

500ml chicken stock

3 tablespoons tamarind paste

This is essentially a rich coconut chicken curry cooked low and slow in the wok so that the meat melts and becomes very tender. Inspired by the rich fusion of cultures in Macau – Portuguese, African, Chinese and Indian – and using tamarind paste borrowed from Africa, it's a great dish for entertaining because you can cook it in advance. Chopping the chicken across the bone adds flavour, but rinse the pieces in cold water afterwards to remove any splintered bits, or ask your butcher to do so.

Serves 6 kcal 726 carbs 66.6g protein 37.0g fat 37.3g

Heat a wok over a high heat until smoking, add the vegetable oil and give it a swirl. Add the chicken and brown for 3–4 minutes. Remove the chicken from the wok and reheat the wok over a medium heat.

To make the curry, add the butter and vegetable oil to the wok and fry the garlic, shallots, onions and curry powder for 2 minutes until the onions are translucent. Add the chicken, desiccated coconut and aubergine slices and stir-fry for 2–3 minutes. Add the coconut milk, chicken stock and tamarind paste and bring to a simmer, then simmer over a medium heat for 35–40 minutes until the chicken is cooked through and falling off the bone.

Meanwhile, cook the potatoes in a pan of boiling salted water for 15 minutes, then drain and set aside.

While the curry is simmering, wash the rice in a sieve until the water runs clear. Place in a medium pot and cover with 600ml water. Bring to the boil, reduce the heat to low, cover the pan and simmer for 15–20 minutes until all the water has been absorbed. Fluff up the grains, cover and keep it warm on the hob.

Add the cooked potatoes to the curry and cook for 10 minutes. Then stir in the broccoli and cook for 2 minutes. Season to taste with salt and white pepper, remove from the heat and serve immediately with the rice.

Prep time: 1 hour marinade
Oven time: 40 mins for the duck

 DF

2 x 400g duck legs

For the marinade
2 garlic cloves, minced
2 tablespoons freshly grated
    peeled ginger
1 tablespoon Shaohsing rice wine
    or dry sherry
1 teaspoon Chinese five-spice
    powder
2 tablespoons runny honey
2 tablespoons hoisin sauce
1 tablespoon dark soy sauce
pinch of salt

For the wontons
peanut oil
about 20–30 wonton wrappers
pinch of salt
pinch of ground white pepper
finely chopped chives

To serve
2–3 tablespoons hoisin sauce
250g strawberries, sliced

For the dressing (optional)
1 tablespoon plum sauce
1 tablespoon hoisin sauce
2 tablespoons olive oil
2 tablespoons lime juice
pinch of caster sugar
1 teaspoon tamari or low-sodium
    light soy sauce

HOISIN DUCK AND STRAWBERRY WOK-FRIED CRISPY WONTON 'TACOS'

I was messing around with wonton wrappers and came up with the idea for turning them into little crispy 'tacos'. Great for gatherings, they're easy to make and can be cooked in advance and assembled when the party gets started. The fresh strawberry slices add a lovely pop of sweetness. Although you need to allow time for prep, they are assembled very quickly.

Serves 4 kcal 477 carbs 46.7g protein 17.2g fat 25g

Place the duck legs in a ziplock bag. Add all the marinade ingredients, turn to coat the legs and marinate in the fridge for at least 1 hour.

Preheat the oven to 180°C, Gas Mark 4. Place the duck legs (and the marinade) round-side up on a roasting tray lined with foil and roast for 40 minutes, then increase the heat to 220°C, Gas Mark 7 and roast for a further 10 minutes until well done. Remove from the oven, transfer to a plate and carefully pour the cooking juices into a heatproof jug. Leave the duck to rest, then shred the meat when cool to the touch (discarding the bones). Keep covered in a warm oven until ready to serve. Mix the cooking juices with the hoisin sauce (to serve) and set aside.

Heat a wok over a high heat and fill to a third of its depth with peanut oil. Heat the oil over a medium-high heat to 150°C, or until a bread cube dropped in the oil turns golden brown in 15 seconds and floats to the surface. Deep-fry the wontons for 40 seconds until golden and crispy. Spoon out onto kitchen paper, then sprinkle with the salt, white pepper and chives and toss to coat.

To serve, top each wonton with some shredded duck, drizzle over the hoisin mixture and garnish with the sliced strawberries and extra chopped chives.

Ching's Tip
Turn this dish into a salad by serving on some watercress – spread the duck on the leaves, top with the hoisin mixture and broken-up pieces of wontons and garnish with strawberries.

5 mins

9 mins

GF DF

SWEET SPICY CHICKEN WITH CRISPY GREEN PEPPERS

450g chicken thighs, boned and
    skinned, sliced into 5mm strips
1 tablespoon chilli bean paste
2 tablespoons cornflour
rapeseed oil, for deep-frying
pinch of salt
1 large white onion, cut into
    half-moon slices
3 long dried red chillies
1 large green pepper, deseeded
    and sliced into 1cm strips
1 tablespoon tamari or low-
    sodium light soy sauce
3 tablespoons sweet chilli sauce
juice of ½ orange
½ teaspoon dark soy sauce
1 spring onion, finely sliced, to
    garnish

**This is one of those quick and delicious easy winner dinners.
Seasoning the chicken with chilli bean paste – a fiery Sichuan
paste of soybeans and chilli that is rich in umami and heat in
equal measure – ensures it has bags of flavour. Then coating
it with a light dusting of cornflour locks in the flavour and the
moisture. Jasmine rice is the perfect accompaniment to soak
up the delish flavours of the sauce.**

**For a vegan version, use sliced king trumpet mushrooms or
sliced fresh shiitake mushrooms and just wok-fry with the
crispy green peppers.**

Serves 2 kcal 648 carbs 48g protein 50g fat 30.8g

Place the chicken strips in a large bowl and season with the chilli
bean paste. Mix well, then add the cornflour and toss until the
chicken has absorbed it.

Heat a wok over a high heat and fill to a third of its depth
with rapeseed oil. Heat the oil to 180°C, or until a bread cube
dropped in the oil turns golden brown in 15 seconds and floats to
the surface. Frying in batches, lower the chicken into the oil and
cook until golden brown, about 5 minutes, then drain on kitchen
paper. Drain the oil through a heatproof colander set over a
heatproof bowl.

Reheat the wok over a high heat and add 1 teaspoon of the oil,
pinch of salt, the onion and dried chillies and wok-fry for a few
seconds to release their aroma. Add the green peppers and
toss-cook for 30 seconds to sear and crisp them at the edges.
Then add the tamari or light soy sauce, sweet chilli sauce, orange
juice and dark soy sauce and bring to a bubble. Add the chicken
and toss together with the peppers to coat well, then serve
immediately with jasmine rice.

CHING'S CHICKEN CHAU CHAU PARIDA

1 tablespoon rapeseed oil

3 garlic cloves, finely chopped

2.5cm piece of fresh ginger, peeled and finely chopped

2 spring onions, sliced into 1cm rounds

2 pinches of salt

1 teaspoon ground turmeric

500g chicken thighs, skinned, boned, sliced into 2.5cm chunks

50ml Shaohsing rice wine or dry sherry

1 tablespoon tamari or low-sodium light soy sauce

1 tablespoon Chinkiang black rice vinegar or balsamic vinegar

3 grinds of cracked black pepper

200g tenderstem broccoli stems, par-boiled for 1 minute

This recipe is inspired by the Macanese 'Chau Chau Parida', a stir-fried dish usually eaten by Chinese mothers to replace the 'yang' energy after giving birth. This is a restorative dish and delicious with some sweet tenderstem broccoli added in. The gingery, warm, savoury and winey notes work well with plain jasmine rice.

Serves 2 kcal 536 carbs 9.5g protein 57.3g fat 30.7g

Heat a wok over a high heat until smoking, add the rapeseed oil and give the oil a swirl. Add the garlic, ginger, spring onions, salt and turmeric and cook for 10 seconds to release their aroma.

Add the chicken pieces and sear on one side for 30 seconds, then toss and cook for 2–3 minutes until browned all over. Before the chicken is completely cooked, add the rice wine or dry sherry. Cook for 1 minute to reduce the wine, then add the tamari or light soy sauce, vinegar and season with the black pepper. Toss in the par-boiled tenderstem broccoli. Remove from the heat and serve with jasmine rice.

10 mins

9 mins

GF DF

OYSTER SAUCE CHICKEN WITH CHINESE LEAF

300g chicken thighs, boned,
    skinned, sliced into 1cm strips
2 spring onions, sliced on the
    angle, to garnish

For the marinade
pinch of salt
pinch of ground white pepper
1 tablespoon oyster sauce
1 tablespoon cornflour

For the stir-fry
2 tablespoons rapeseed oil
1 garlic clove, finely chopped
2.5cm piece of fresh ginger,
    peeled and grated
1 red chilli, deseeded and finely
    chopped
1 tablespoon Shaohsing rice wine
    or dry sherry
150g Chinese leaf, sliced into
    5cm chunks

For the sauce
50ml hot vegetable stock
2 tablespoons tamari or low-
    sodium light soy sauce
1 teaspoon toasted sesame oil

This is a Beijing-meets-Canton-style home-wokked dish. Whenever I eat Chinese leaf, it reminds me of the Shandong province and their obsession with leafy cabbage vegetables – a symbol of peasant food. Oyster sauce was created in Guangdong and is a secret umami savoury weapon I cannot live without in my store cupboard. The oyster sauce makes the chicken super moreish and works so well with the Chinese leaf, which lends a delicious sweet bite once softened. The wok juices are perfect drizzled over jasmine rice.

If you're vegan, you can use firm tofu instead of the chicken, and vegetarian oyster sauce, and it would be equally delish.

Serves 2 kcal 437 carbs 18.8g protein 41.7g fat 36g

Put the chicken and all the ingredients for the marinade in a bowl and turn to coat.

Heat a wok over a high heat until smoking, then add 1 tablespoon of the rapeseed oil and give it a swirl. Add the garlic, ginger and chilli and stir-fry for a few seconds, then add the chicken. Wok-fry the chicken for 2 minutes until it starts to caramelise and turn opaque. Add the rice wine or dry sherry and deglaze the wok. Cook for another 2 minutes until the chicken is cooked through. Spoon out onto a plate.

Reheat the wok over a high heat until smoking, then add the remaining rapeseed oil and give it a swirl. Add the Chinese leaf and stir-fry for 1 minute, then add about 2 tablespoons cold water to help create some steam to cook the leaves. Pour in all the sauce ingredients and bring to the boil. Once the Chinese leaf has wilted, spoon out onto serving plates, top with the chicken pieces and garnish with the spring onions. Serve with jasmine rice.

10 mins

25 mins

DF

STEAMED SICHUAN HOT AND SOUR CHICKEN

4 boneless, skinless chicken thighs

2 tablespoons Shaohsing rice wine or dry sherry

pinch of salt

pinch of ground white pepper

1 tablespoon cornflour

2.5cm piece of fresh ginger, peeled and sliced into matchsticks

2 large spring onions, sliced lengthways

200g tenderstem broccoli, sliced on an angle

For the dressing

2 tablespoons tamari or low-sodium light soy sauce

1 teaspoon toasted sesame oil

2 garlic cloves, finely chopped

2.5cm piece of fresh ginger, peeled and finely grated

1 red chilli, deseeded and finely chopped

1 tablespoon Sichuan mustard pickle in chilli oil, finely chopped

3 tablespoons rapeseed oil

1 teaspoon dark soy sauce

2 tablespoons rice vinegar

pinch of soft brown sugar

This is a super healthy and easy recipe. The dressing combines raw garlic and ginger and is pungent, bold and full of flavour – if you can't get the Sichuan mustard pickle, just do without, though if you can it's worth every bite.

Serves 2 kcal 559 carbs 18.8g protein 41.7g fat 36g

Place the chicken in a heatproof bowl (that can fit inside a steamer) and drizzle with the rice wine or dry sherry. Season the chicken with the salt, white pepper and cornflour, then place the ginger matchsticks on top of the chicken and drape half of the spring onion slices over.

Place the bowl in a bamboo steamer, cover with a lid and steam over a wok of simmering water (making sure the water does not touch the base of the steamer) for 15–20 minutes (depending on the size of the thighs), or until the chicken is cooked through. Check the water level during cooking and top up with boiling water if necessary.

Place all the dressing ingredients in a bowl and stir to combine.

In a separate pan, bring 750ml water to the boil, add the broccoli and blanch for 2 minutes. Remove and drain, then transfer to a serving plate and drizzle with 1 tablespoon of the dressing.

Remove the chicken from the steamer. Pour any cooking juices into the dressing and mix. Transfer the chicken to a chopping board and chop into long, rectangular chunks. Place over the broccoli and spoon over the remaining dressing. Garnish with the remaining spring onion slices and serve immediately.

10 mins

8 mins

GF DF

THAI-INSPIRED CHICKEN COCONUT BROTH

400g boneless, skinless chicken
    thighs, sliced into 2.5cm
    chunks
pinch of salt
pinch of ground white pepper
1 teaspoon cornflour
1 tablespoon rapeseed oil
2 stalks of lemongrass, sliced into
    2.5cm pieces
500ml hot vegetable stock
100ml coconut milk
1 kaffir lime leaf, whole
2 ripe tomatoes, quartered,
    skin on
200g oyster mushrooms
2 tablespoons fish sauce
juice of 1 lime
½ teaspoon caster sugar
coriander, to garnish

This is a healthy light coconut chicken broth dinner.
Sometimes I love a soup for dinner, especially if I've had a
heavy day of eating. For me, the key to keeping the chicken
succulent and moist is to wok-fry and seal it first. Then add
all the rest of the ingredients. It's quick and makes a delicious
light supper.

Vegans can substitute the chicken for extra meaty oyster
mushrooms and the fish sauce for vegetarian oyster sauce.

Serves 2 kcal 520 carbs 13.2g protein 46.6g fat 34.7g

Put the chicken in a bowl and season with the salt, white pepper
and cornflour.

Heat a wok over a high heat until smoking, add the rapeseed oil
and give the oil a swirl. Add the lemongrass and toss for a few
seconds to release its aroma. Add the chicken and sear for a few
seconds, then cook, tossing, for 2–3 minutes until almost cooked
through. Add the hot vegetable stock, coconut milk, lime leaf,
tomatoes and mushrooms. Season with the fish sauce, lime juice
and caster sugar and bring to the boil. Then turn the heat down
to medium and simmer for another 2 minutes. Take off the heat,
garnish with coriander and serve.

20 mins

5–6 mins

GF DF

CHICKEN, SHRIMP AND MUSHROOM CONGEE

1 tablespoon rapeseed oil

1 tablespoon finely grated peeled fresh ginger

2 boneless, skinless chicken thighs, finely diced

1 tablespoon Shaohsing rice wine, dry sherry or vegetable stock

100g dried Chinese shrimps, soaked in hot water for 15 minutes, drained and finely chopped

4 dried Chinese mushrooms, soaked in hot water for 20 minutes, drained, stalks discarded, diced

1 tablespoon tamari or low-sodium light soy sauce

1 tablespoon oyster sauce

pinch of salt

pinch of ground white pepper

1 tablespoon toasted sesame oil

1 quantity Classic Plain Congee 'Zhou' (see page 52)

handful of baby spinach leaves, rolled up and sliced

handful of finely chopped coriander

1 spring onion, finely chopped

This surf 'n' turf combination of chicken and seafood is so Asian. I love pork congee but chicken works just as well too. The trick is to use chicken thighs off the bone, diced very finely. Use dried shrimps as well, as they are full of flavour. This is a flavourful and delicious dish and my own proud invention. I hope you enjoy it!

Serves 6 kcal 310 carbs 44g protein 19.9g fat 7.4g

Heat a wok over a high heat until smoking, add the rapeseed oil and give the oil a swirl. Add the ginger and chicken and stir-fry quickly for 3 minutes until the chicken is almost cooked. Add the rice wine, dry sherry or vegetable stock, the Chinese shrimps and mushrooms and stir-fry until fragrant and the chicken is cooked through.

Season with the tamari or light soy sauce, oyster sauce, salt, white pepper and sesame oil. Add this to the congee and stir well. Check the seasoning and season further to your taste. Stir the spinach, chopped coriander and spring onion through and serve immediately.

2 mins

3–4 mins

GF DF

CHICKEN WITH GINGER CHOI SUM AND GOJI BERRIES

For the chicken

250g boneless chicken thighs, skinned and sliced into 2.5cm chunks

pinch of dried chilli flakes

½ teaspoon Chinese five-spice powder

pinch of salt

pinch of ground white pepper

1 tablespoon cornflour

1 tablespoon rapeseed oil

2 tablespoons Shaohsing rice wine or dry sherry

1 tablespoon tamari or low-sodium light soy sauce

1 teaspoon toasted sesame oil

small handful of dried goji berries, soaked in warm water for 5 minutes, drained

For the stir-fry

1 tablespoon rapeseed oil

pinch of salt

2.5cm piece of fresh ginger, peeled and grated

400g Chinese choi sum (or tenderstem broccoli or pak choy), washed and sliced into 5cm pieces

50ml hot vegetable stock

Before she turned veggie, my mother used to make steamed Shaohsing rice wine chicken with goji berries and ginger. I have turned it into a stir fry because I love the wok-seared taste of the chicken when it cooks in the wok together with the choi sum (though pak choy would be delicious too), and the bitter sweetness of the goji berries. A quick, simple, healthy recipe that is energising and full of goodness.

You can make this one vegan by substituting meaty oyster mushrooms for the chicken.

Serves 2 kcal 437 carbs 26.9g protein 36.9g fat 21.1g

Season the chicken with the dried chilli flakes, Chinese five-spice powder, salt and white pepper, and dust with the cornflour. Set aside.

For the stir-fry, heat a wok over a high heat until smoking, then add the rapeseed oil and a pinch of salt. Give it a swirl. Add the ginger and stir-fry for a few seconds to release its aroma. Add the Chinese choi sum (or broccoli or pak choy) and stir-fry for 1 minute, tossing it in the wok. Add the hot stock around the edges, then transfer to a warm serving plate.

Finish the chicken. Reheat the wok until smoking, add the rapeseed oil and give the oil a swirl. Add the seasoned chicken pieces and sear for 30 seconds, then toss to turn and cook the chicken for 2 minutes over a high heat. Add the rice wine or dry sherry and cook, tossing and stirring, for another 2 minutes until the chicken is cooked through. Season with the tamari or light soy sauce and sesame oil. Stir in the goji berries and give it one last toss. Spoon out on top of the choi sum and serve immediately. Perfect with jasmine rice.

10 mins

15 mins

DF

CHILLI CHICKEN AND CHINESE BROCCOLI NOODLE SOUP

150g dried buckwheat or wheat flour noodles
1 teaspoon toasted sesame oil
1 tablespoon rapeseed oil
few pinches of cracked salt
2 small garlic cloves, roughly chopped
2.5cm piece of fresh ginger, peeled and finely grated
1 large red cayenne chilli, deseeded and sliced
2 boneless skinless chicken breasts, sliced thinly on the angle
1 tablespoon Shaohsing rice wine or dry sherry
1 tablespoon chilli bean paste
1 tablespoon vegetable bouillon powder
2 tablespoons Chinkiang black rice vinegar or balsamic vinegar
1 tablespoon tamari or low-sodium light soy sauce
pinch of soft brown sugar
1 teaspoon toasted sesame oil
150g gai lan (Chinese broccoli), tenderstem broccoli or pak choy, sliced on the angle into 2.5cm pieces
1 spring onion, sliced on a deep angle, to garnish

The ginger and chillies give this a perfect warming heat, and the broccoli (whether you choose a Chinese or Western variety) is full of antioxidants. I prefer thin rather than thick noodles but it's up to you.

You can make this dish vegan by substituting sliced fresh shiitake mushrooms and smoked tofu for the chicken.

Serves 2 kcal 568 carbs 64.7g protein 50.2g fat 11.2g

Cook the noodles according to the packet instructions, then drain and dress with toasted sesame oil.

Heat a wok over a high heat until smoking, add the rapeseed oil and give the oil a swirl. Add the salt to dissolve in the oil. Add the garlic, ginger and chilli and stir-fry for a few seconds to release their aroma. Add the chicken slices and sear for 1 minute, then toss and stir-fry for 2–3 minutes. Season with the rice wine or dry sherry, then add 1.2 litres boiling water, the chilli bean paste, bouillon powder, vinegar, tamari or light soy sauce, brown sugar and sesame oil. Stir well and bring the broth to a simmer. Drop in the broccoli or pak choy and cook for 1 minute.

Divide the noodles between two bowls, pour in the broth, garnish with the spring onion and serve immediately.

20 mins

5-6 mins

GF DF

FIVE-SPICE SAUCY CHICKEN STIR-FRY

280g boneless, skinless chicken thighs, sliced into 1cm slices
pinch of cracked salt
pinch of cracked black pepper
1 teaspoon Chinese five-spice powder
1 tablespoon cornflour
1 tablespoon rapeseed oil
2 garlic cloves, finely chopped
2.5cm piece of fresh ginger, peeled and grated
1 fat jalapeño chilli, deseeded and finely chopped
100g Chantenay carrots or baby carrots, peeled and tops trimmed
1 tablespoon tamari or low-sodium light soy sauce
5 baby leeks, cut on an angle into 1cm slices
8 Savoy cabbage leaves, shredded

For the sauce
150ml cold vegetable stock or chicken stock
2 tablespoons tamari or low-sodium light soy sauce
1 teaspoon dark soy sauce
1 tablespoon cornflour

This is my take on bringing the flavours of a Sunday roast right into a wok fry! Call me crazy but this dish is super delicious and the sauce delivers on that moreish 'chickeny gravy' flavour – as they say, it's all gravy baby and this one happens to be laced with delicious five-spice.

You can vegan-fy this recipe by using a combination of meaty oyster mushrooms and sliced shiitake mushrooms instead of the chicken.

Serves 2 kcal 545 carbs 34.7g protein 34.2g fat 31.5g

Combine all the ingredients for the sauce in a small jug and mix well.

Put the chicken in a bowl, then season with the salt, black pepper, five-spice powder and cornflour and toss together. Set aside.

Heat a wok over a high heat until smoking, add the rapeseed oil and give it a swirl. Add the garlic, ginger and chilli and stir for a few seconds to release their aroma. Then add the carrots and stir-fry for just over 1 minute. Add the chicken slices and sear for a few seconds, then toss together for 3–4 minutes. Season with the tamari or light soy sauce, then add the leeks and cabbage and stir-fry together for 1 minute.

Add the sauce and bring to a bubble to thicken. Stir and mix well. Transfer to serving plates and serve with boiled or roast new potatoes and jasmine rice.

10 mins

7-8 mins

GF DF

MALAYSIAN-STYLE FRIED CHICKEN WITH OKRA

For the spice paste
2 garlic cloves, crushed
2.5cm piece of fresh ginger, peeled and grated
½ teaspoon ground cumin
½ teaspoon ground fennel
½ teaspoon ground coriander
½ teaspoon ground cloves
½ teaspoon ground cinnamon
2 green cardamom pods
2 curry leaves
1 teaspoon ground turmeric
1 teaspoon dried chilli flakes
pinch of salt

For the stir-fry
400g boneless, skinless chicken thighs, sliced into 2.5cm chunks
1 tablespoon rapeseed oil
50ml coconut milk
100g okra, sliced in half on the angle
2 tablespoons vegetable stock
pinch of salt
pinch of soft brown sugar
juice of 1 lime

This includes one of my pop-in-law's spice mixes that he uses for his famous curry dishes. I've turned it on its head by using it to make a wok-curried, stir-fry supper with chicken and okra. If you're not a fan of okra, then leave it out.

For a vegan version, use meaty oyster mushrooms and tofu instead of the chicken.

Serves 4 kcal 226 carbs 2.1g protein 23.1g fat 16.5g

Using a stick blender or a special spice blender/clean coffee grinder, grind all the ingredients for the spice paste with 50ml water. Add to the chicken in a bowl and toss to mix well.

Heat a wok over a high heat until smoking, add the rapeseed oil and swirl it around. Stir-fry the chicken for 5 minutes until cooked through, then add the coconut milk and cook until the chicken has absorbed it and the sauce has reduced down. Add the okra and vegetable stock and toss for 1 minute. Season with the salt, brown sugar and lime juice. Serve with jasmine rice.

TURMERIC CHICKEN PEPPER STIR-FRY

½ teaspoon ground turmeric

½ teaspoon dried chilli flakes

½ teaspoon ground coriander

2 boneless chicken breasts, skinned and sliced into 1cm strips

1 tablespoon rapeseed oil

2.5cm piece of fresh ginger, peeled and grated

1 tablespoon Shaohsing rice wine or dry sherry

2 tablespoons vegetable stock

1 red pepper, deseeded and cut into julienne strips

1 green pepper, deseeded and cut into julienne strips

small handful of mangetout

1 tablespoon tamari or low-sodium light soy sauce

juice of 1 lemon

25g salted cashew nuts, crushed in a pestle and mortar or roughly chopped

You can load as much crunchy veg as you wish into this spiced chicken stir-fry. Simple and quick, it packs in protein, veg and flavour for an easy one-wok dinner!

Serves 2 kcal 375 carbs 15.5g protein 43.8g fat 15.5g

Combine the turmeric, chilli flakes and ground coriander in a bowl. Add the chicken strips and toss to mix well.

Heat a wok over a high heat until smoking, add the rapeseed oil and give the oil a swirl to coat the sides of the wok. Add the ginger, fry for a few seconds, then add the spiced chicken slices and sear to release their aroma and flavour into the oil for a few seconds. Flip the chicken and toss for 3–4 minutes so that it colours and caramelises at the edges. Add the rice wine or dry sherry followed by the stock. Quickly add the red and green pepper strips and mangetout and stir-fry for 1 minute.

Season with the tamari or light soy sauce and the lemon juice. Tip in the cashew nuts and eat immediately.

PORK, BEEF

& LAMB

10 mins

5 mins

GF DF

WOK-FRIED BEEF IN CHILLI SAUCE WITH CORIANDER

1 tablespoon rapeseed oil

1 garlic clove, crushed

200g beef fillet, sliced into strips

1 tablespoon Shaohsing rice wine or dry sherry

100g mangetout or sugarsnap peas

225g can sliced water chestnuts, drained

chopped coriander, to garnish

For the sauce

80g unsalted peanuts, crushed until smooth, or use smooth peanut butter

1 teaspoon Sichuan pepper (toasted and ground)

1 teaspoon runny honey

2 tablespoons tamari or low-sodium light soy sauce

1 teaspoon chilli oil

1 teaspoon toasted sesame oil

1 teaspoon Chinkiang black rice vinegar or balsamic vinegar

1 teaspoon chilli bean paste or your favourite chilli sauce

pinch of salt

I love simple, easy, straightforward suppers such as this one. Go wild like Tom Cruise in *Cocktail* when creating the sauce – infuse, shake, juggle and stir!

This dish is perfect with plain jasmine rice and extra steamed greens on the side. For vegans, substitute smoked tofu slices and sliced fresh shiitake mushrooms for the beef, and golden syrup for the honey.

Serves 2   kcal 498   carbs 18g   protein 36.3g   fat 31.4g

Combine all the ingredients for the sauce in a small bowl and mix well. Set aside.

Heat a wok over a high heat until smoking, add the rapeseed oil and give the oil a swirl. Add the garlic and fry for a few seconds, then add the beef strips and sear for a few seconds on one side, then flip over. Season with the rice wine or dry sherry. Add the mangetout or sugarsnap peas and water chestnuts, and toss for 1 minute. Pour in the sauce and toss together well until all the ingredients have been coated. Garnish with chopped coriander and serve immediately.

BEEF AND PEA WONTONS

16 wonton wrappers or pasta or ravioli wrappers

For the filling
50g minced beef
50g frozen peas, defrosted
1 teaspoon freshly grated peeled ginger
1 teaspoon Shaohsing rice wine or dry sherry
1 spring onion, finely chopped
1 teaspoon vegetable bouillon powder
pinch of salt
pinch of ground white pepper

To serve
good shop-bought or homemade gravy of your choice
chiu chow chilli oil
handful of crushed unsalted peanuts

*per wonton

When I'm in need of comfort, these are my go-to wontons, particularly as they are so easy to make – just wrap and twist, no need for fiddling around with pleats. I use minced beef in these dumplings and peas for texture, and I like to serve them with good old English gravy and a splash of Chinese chilli oil. Wok's not to love? A bit of British Chineseness never hurt anyone.

If you're vegan, use vegan wrappers and rehydrated soy mince instead of minced beef and then follow the rest of the recipe.

Makes 16 kcal 41 carbs 6g protein 2.2g fat 0.9g*

Mix together all the ingredients for the filling in a bowl.

Take a teaspoon of the filling and place in the centre of a wonton wrapper. Gather the four sides and pinch and twist to seal. Repeat with the rest of the filling and wonton wrappers.

Steam or boil in a wok for 8 minutes (see tip). Remove and pour on lashings of gravy. Spoon over some chiu chow chilli oil and garnish with crushed peanuts. Serve immediately.

Ching's Tip
Or deep-fry in hot oil at 180°C for 2-3 minutes until the wontons are golden and the inside is cooked. Drain on kitchen paper before serving.

15 mins

7 mins

DF

BEEF AND MUSHROOM BEIJING-STYLE WHEAT FLOUR PANCAKES

1 x 300g sirloin steak, cut into 1cm dice
pinch of salt
pinch of ground white pepper
1 teaspoon Shaohsing rice wine or dry sherry
1 tablespoon oyster sauce
1 tablespoon rapeseed oil
5 dried Chinese mushrooms, soaked in hot water for 15 minutes, drained, stalks discarded, finely diced
1 tablespoon tamari or low-sodium light soy sauce
1 teaspoon toasted sesame oil
2 Chinese garlic chives or spring onions, sliced into 2mm pieces
10 shop-bought Chinese wheat flour pancakes
small handful of toasted sesame seeds, to garnish

This makes a great light snack or supper or delicious party food. The meaty Chinese mushrooms add bite and texture and the oyster sauce gives a rich umami flavour to the beef. Easy and quick – perfect for a lazy wok day!

If you are vegan, you can use small pieces of smoked tofu and vegetarian oyster sauce instead of oyster sauce.

Serves 2 kcal 473 carbs 32.8g protein 41.6g fat 19.2g

Season the beef with the salt, white pepper, rice wine or dry sherry and the oyster sauce and rub in.

Heat a wok over a high heat until smoking, add the rapeseed oil and give the oil a swirl. Add the beef and fry for a few seconds until browned at the edges, then add the mushrooms and toss for a few minutes until tender. Season with the tamari or light soy sauce and sesame oil, then sprinkle in the garlic chives or spring onions. Transfer to a plate, cover and keep warm.

Wipe the wok with kitchen paper, half fill with water and bring to a simmer. Place the wheat flour pancakes on a heatproof plate lined with greaseproof paper, then put on a rack set over the wok and steam for 4 minutes over a high heat, then remove to warm plates and cover with foil.

Spoon some of the beef and mushroom mixture onto each pancake, garnish with toasted sesame seeds and eat immediately.

PEARLY BEEF BALLS

15 mins

20 mins

DF

100g glutinous rice
dried goji berries

For the beef balls
400g minced beef
pinch of salt
pinch of ground white pepper
1 tablespoon Shaohsing rice wine
    or dry sherry
50g French beans, finely diced
1 teaspoon vegetable bouillon
    powder
1 teaspoon toasted sesame oil
1 teaspoon cornflour

For the dipping sauce
1 tablespoon black rice vinegar
peeled fresh ginger matchsticks

Although this is quick to cook once everything is prepared, you need to soak the glutinous rice for 1½ hours.

This is my variation of the Cantonese classic, which is usually made with pork instead of beef. But the Chinese use meat very sparingly and a little goes a long way! These delightful beauties are perfect when steamed. If you cannot get glutinous rice, use sushi rice instead.

Serves 2 kcal 488 carbs 32.8g protein 41.6g fat 19.2g

Wash the glutinous rice until the water runs clear, then soak in fresh cold water for 1½ hours. Drain.

Mix together all the ingredients for the beef balls. Shape the mixture into about 12 balls the size of small golf balls, then roll in the drained rice to coat and place in a bamboo steamer. Top each one with a goji berry, cover and steam over a wok halfway filled with boiling water over a high heat for 15–20 minutes until the beef is cooked and the rice is al dente but pearlescent.

Serve with the black rice vinegar dipping sauce, adding the ginger matchsticks to it.

10 mins

5 mins

GF DF

FIVE-SPICE PORK AND BLACK BEAN WOOD EAR WITH SPRING ONIONS

1 tablespoon rapeseed oil

2.5cm piece of fresh ginger, peeled and grated

1 red chilli, deseeded and finely chopped

200g pork fillet, sliced into 5mm strips, lightly dusted with cornflour

pinch of Chinese five-spice powder

1 teaspoon dark soy sauce

1 tablespoon Shaohsing rice wine or dry sherry

100g dried wood ear mushrooms, (soaked in hot water for 20 minutes), sliced into strips, or canned bamboo shoots

1 teaspoon black bean paste

100ml hot vegetable stock

1 tablespoon tamari or low-sodium light soy sauce

1 tablespoon cornflour, blended with 2 tablespoons cold water

2 spring onions, sliced on the angle, to garnish

I'm a huge fan of dried Chinese wood ear mushrooms, which, when soaked, double in size and become a delicious crunchy addition to any stir fry. They are only available in Chinese supermarkets, but these days you can order anything online. They are so full of nutritious goodness that my mother blends them into a smoothie-like drink – apparently their bouncy texture replicates collagen and is good for the skin (it also helps the digestion).

For vegans, substitute the pork with smoked tofu or a medley of meaty mushrooms. Enjoy!

Serves 2 kcal 370 carbs 42.8g protein 27.9g fat 10.8g

Heat a wok over a high heat until smoking, add the rapeseed oil and give the oil a swirl. Add the ginger and chilli and toss for a few seconds, then add the pork and sear on one side. Season with the five-spice powder, dark soy sauce and rice wine or dry sherry and cook for 1 minute until cooked through. Add the wood ear mushrooms or bamboo shoots, the black bean paste, vegetable stock and tamari or light soy sauce and bring the sauce to the boil. Stir in the blended cornflour and quickly stir together (the cornflour thickens quickly). Garnish with the spring onions and serve immediately with jasmine rice.

5 mins

+ 20 mins for pre-cooking rice

5 mins

GF DF

BEEF AND SPINACH RICE SOUP

1 tablespoon rapeseed oil

2.5cm piece of fresh ginger, peeled and sliced into matchsticks

100g sirloin steak, finely diced

½ teaspoon dark soy sauce

pinch of Chinese five-spice powder

1 tablespoon Shaohsing rice wine or dry sherry

500ml hot vegetable stock

200g cooked jasmine rice

1 tablespoon tamari or low-sodium light soy sauce

pinch of ground white pepper

1–2 teaspoons toasted sesame oil

1 tablespoon cornflour, blended with 2 tablespoons cold water

100g baby leaf spinach

1 spring onion, finely sliced, to garnish

This quick and heart-warming dish starts off as a stir-fry, and then when you add cooked rice, veggie stock and seasonings, it turns into a soupy congee, which is comfort food for me. You can make it chunkier by adding more rice and less stock, or if you like a brothy kind of dish, add more veggie stock. Either way, the wilted spinach will give you a delicious hit of green.

If you are vegan, replace the beef with mushrooms and smoked tofu.

Serves 2 kcal 315 carbs 37.4g protein 17.1g fat 12.1g

Heat a wok over a high heat until smoking, add the rapeseed oil and give the oil a swirl. Add the ginger and toss for a few seconds, then add the diced steak and sear on one side. Flip the meat over, season with the dark soy sauce and five-spice powder and cook for 1 minute. Add the rice wine or dry sherry, then pour in the hot vegetable stock, 100ml boiling water and the cooked jasmine rice. Season with the tamari or light soy sauce, white pepper and sesame oil, then stir in the blended cornflour and bring to the boil. Stir in the baby spinach to wilt, then garnish with the spring onion and serve immediately.

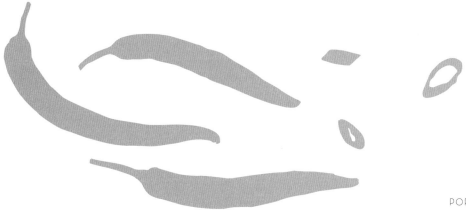

10 mins

45 mins

DF

OXTAIL AND TURNIP NOODLE SOUP (NUOROMEIN)

2 tablespoons rapeseed oil
5 whole baby shallots, peeled
500g oxtail, chopped into 2.5cm chunks
1 whole fat garlic clove, peeled
1 red chilli, sliced
2.5cm piece of fresh ginger, peeled
1 star anise
½ daikon (15cm), cut into 2.5cm chunks
1 small carrot, sliced in half lengthways, then cut into 5mm half-moon chunks
600ml chicken stock
1 tablespoon Shaohsing rice wine or dry sherry
1 tablespoon chilli bean paste
1 teaspoon chilli sauce
1 teaspoon dark soy sauce
2 teaspoons soft brown sugar
2 heads of baby pak choy, sliced down the middle
200g dried flat wheat flour or udon noodles

For the garnish

2 spring onions, sliced into strips and soaked in iced water for 5 minutes to curl, drained
small bunch of coriander, stems and leaves sliced

I love the warmth and comforting flavour of this broth alongside the slippery wheat flour or udon noodles. It makes an easy and satisfying supper. For those who like a 'cleaner' broth, blanch the oxtail in boiling water for 10 minutes before cooking to remove any impurities. But if you are short on time, a good wash beforehand should be enough.

Serves 2 kcal 752 carbs 83.3g protein 32.1g fat 8.9g

Heat a wok over a high heat, pour in 1 tablespoon of the rapeseed oil and give the oil a swirl. Add the baby shallots and brown for less than 1 minute. Add the oxtail chunks and brown each side for 30 seconds, then stir in the garlic, chilli, ginger, star anise, daikon and carrot. Pour in 300ml water and the chicken stock and season with the rice wine or dry sherry, the chilli bean paste, chilli sauce, dark soy sauce and soft brown sugar. Cover and simmer over a medium heat for 45 minutes.

Bring a large pot of water to the boil and blanch the pak choy for less than 30 seconds. Lift out, drain well and set aside. Add the noodles to the boiling water and cook according to the packet instructions, then drain and dress with the remaining rapeseed oil and toss together well.

Before serving, check the seasoning of the broth and add more soy sauce to taste, if preferred. Portion the noodles into two bowls, then divide the broth between the bowls and add the pak choy. Garnish with the spring onions and coriander and serve immediately.

15 mins

5 mins

GF DF

CHUNKY BLACK PEPPER HONEY BEEF

500g sirloin steak, cut into
    5mm-thick cubes
pinch of salt
pinch of cracked black pepper
1 tablespoon tamari or low-
    sodium light soy sauce
small handful of coriander
    leaves, to garnish

For the stir-fry
1 tablespoon rapeseed oil
1 garlic clove, whole, peeled and
    crushed
2 large white onions, cut into
    5mm-thick chunks
1 tablespoon Shaohsing rice wine
    or dry sherry
2 red peppers, deseeded and
    cut into 5mm-thick chunks

For the sauce
100ml cold chicken stock
1 tablespoon oyster sauce
1 tablespoon tamari or low-
    sodium light soy sauce
1 teaspoon dark soy sauce
4 tablespoons runny honey
½ teaspoon cracked black
    pepper
1 tablespoon cornflour

This is super quick to make – you can have all the ingredients pre-prepped and then just wok it up at the last minute so that it's piping hot. I promise you this will be a winner with your family and friends.

Serves 4 kcal 333 carbs 33.5g protein 32.1g fat 8.9g

Put the beef in a bowl with the salt, black pepper and tamari or light soy sauce and mix well.

Put all the ingredients for the sauce into a small jug and stir to mix well.

For the stir-fry, heat a wok over a high heat until smoking, add the rapeseed oil and give the oil a swirl. Add the garlic and cook for a few seconds, then add the onions and stir-fry until translucent. Add the beef chunks and sear on one side for 20 seconds, then flip the meat over and cook to your liking (for best results cook to medium). Then season with the rice wine or dry sherry. Add the red peppers and toss for 30 seconds until slightly softened. Remove the beef, onions and red peppers and set aside on a plate.

Pour the sauce into the wok and reduce until sticky. Quickly return the beef and vegetables to the wok and gently toss together well. Garnish with the coriander and serve with jasmine rice and Garlic Wok Tossed Baby Pak Choy (see page 76).

CHING'S MACANESE MINCHI

For the rice
350g jasmine rice
400ml chicken stock

For the roasted oyster mushrooms
200g oyster mushrooms
1–2 tablespoons olive oil
1–2 large pinches of salt
2 large pinches of cracked black pepper
2 large pinches of dried chilli flakes

For the potatoes
500ml litre sunflower oil
500g baby potatoes, scrubbed, left unpeeled and cut into 1cm dice

For the pork
1 tablespoon rapeseed oil
1 large white onion, diced
2 bay leaves
1 garlic clove, finely chopped
500g lean minced pork
1 tablespoon Shaohsing rice wine or dry sherry
1–2 tablespoons oyster sauce
1–2 tablespoons light soy sauce
1–2 tablespoons Worcestershire sauce

>

contd overleaf

This is another dish that takes slightly longer to cook, but it's well worth the effort. Macanese minchi is traditionally wok-fried pork with some soy and fried potatoes served with runny fried eggs on top – pure comfort food! It is utterly delicious when served with jasmine rice. I've gone a little step further and added oven-roasted mushrooms. It's so good you'll want to have it every weekend.

For vegans, use rehydrated soy mince instead of minced pork, mushroom sauce instead of oyster sauce, vegetable stock instead of chicken stock, and then just omit the fried eggs.

Serves 4 kcal 811 carbs 102g protein 44.8g fat 28.5g

Wash the rice until the water runs clear. Place in a medium saucepan, add the chicken stock and 300ml water and bring to the boil. Once the water is boiling, turn the heat to low, cover with a lid and cook for 15–20 minutes until the rice is fluffy.

Meanwhile, preheat the oven to 180°C, Gas Mark 4. Put the oyster mushrooms on a roasting tray, drizzle with the olive oil and season with the salt, black pepper and chilli flakes. Place in the oven and roast for 5–6 minutes, then turn the oven down to low to keep warm.

To cook the potatoes, heat the sunflower oil in a wok or medium saucepan to 180°C, or until a bread cube dropped in the oil turns golden brown in 15 seconds and floats to the surface. Carefully lower the potato cubes into the oil and fry for 5 minutes until crisp and golden on the edges and soft on the inside. (You may have to do this in batches.) Drain on kitchen paper. When all the potatoes are cooked, drain the last batch and the oil into a steel colander set over a heatproof bowl. Keep the oil to use again.

Heat the wok again over a high heat until smoking, add the rapeseed oil and give it a swirl. Fry the onion until translucent, then add the bay leaves and garlic followed by the minced pork. Sear and brown the pork for 45 seconds, then stir-fry to cook it.

1 teaspoon dark soy sauce
pinch of ground white pepper
(optional)

For the fried eggs
1 tablespoon rapeseed oil
4 eggs
pinch of salt
pinch of ground white pepper

2 large spring onions, sliced into
1cm rounds, to garnish

Before the pork is completely cooked, add the rice wine or dry sherry and season to taste with the oyster sauce, light soy sauce, Worcestershire sauce and dark soy sauce. Add a pinch of white pepper here, if you like. Toss well until the seasoning has coated the pork. Add the fried potatoes and toss together for 1 minute. Season further to taste, if desired, then transfer to a warmed plate and keep to one side.

Cook the eggs. Fire up a frying pan, add the rapeseed oil and give it a swirl. Crack in the eggs and fry over a medium heat for 1 minute, until the bottoms are crispy but the egg yolks are still runny on the top. Season with the salt and white pepper.

Remove the mushrooms from the oven.

Place some rice in the centre of a large serving plate. Pour the minced pork and potato (minchi) over the top, arrange the mushrooms around the sides and lay the fried eggs over the top. Garnish with a sprinkle of spring onions and serve immediately.

Ching's Tip (optional)
Serve with some sliced raw red cabbage seasoned with lemon juice, salt, black pepper and olive oil.

10–12 mins

3 mins

DF

CHING'S CHAR SIU BACON AND SHRIMP RICE NOODLES

For the noodles
100g dried folded flat rice
noodles
1 teaspoon toasted sesame oil

For the char siu bacon and
brown shrimp topping
1 tablespoon rapeseed oil
1 tablespoon freshly grated
peeled ginger
60g beech-smoked bacon
lardons, finely chopped
1 tablespoon char siu sauce
1 teaspoon dark soy sauce
70g cooked baby brown shrimps

To serve and for the garnish
70g blanched beansprouts
1 teaspoon tamari or low-sodium
light soy sauce
1 teaspoon Oriental sesame
dressing
2 spring onions, finely chopped

Like all noodles, rice noodles have little flavour themselves, but one thing that makes them more delicious than other noodles (and write to me if you disagree) is that they are incredible at absorbing flavours – as in a delicious pad Thai or Vietnamese pho. In this recipe, they are served plain but topped with a shrimpy-porky stir-fry topped with beansprouts and spring onions – it makes the perfect quick dinner all year round, plus it's super healthy too.

Serves 2 kcal 404 carbs 50.2g protein 19.7g fat 14.7g

Bring 1 litre water to the boil in a pan, add the noodles and cook for 10–12 minutes until al dente. Drain under cold water, drizzle the sesame oil over and toss together to prevent the noodles from sticking. Set aside.

Meanwhile, heat a wok over a high heat until smoking, add the rapeseed oil and give it a swirl. Add the ginger and stir-fry for a few seconds, then add the lardons and cook for 2 minutes until browning at the edges. Add the char siu sauce and toss for 30 seconds, then add the dark soy sauce and cook for 30 seconds. Add the brown shrimps and stir-fry for another 30 seconds.

To serve, place the noodles on a serving plate, top with the blanched beansprouts, then drizzle on the tamari light soy sauce and sesame dressing. Arrange the char siu lardons and shrimps on top, garnish with the spring onions and serve immediately.

10 mins

5 mins

+ 20 minutes to cook the rice

GF DF

MACANESE-STYLE FRIED RICE – PORTUGUESE CHOURIÇO, BABY SCALLOPS AND CORIANDER

200g jasmine rice

2 tablespoons vegetable oil

2 garlic cloves, finely chopped

2 shallots, finely chopped

½ medium jalapeño chilli, deseeded and finely chopped

3 small spring onions, sliced into 1cm rounds

50g Portuguese black Iberian chouriço or Spanish chorizo, diced

120g baby scallops, cleaned

1 tablespoon Shaohsing rice wine or dry sherry

2-3 tablespoons tamari or low-sodium light soy sauce

pinch of salt

pinch of ground white pepper

juice of 1 large lemon

small handful of coriander leaves and stems sliced

The Macanese cuisine is a fusion of Portuguese and Chinese. The Portuguese way of making seafood rice is to cook it risotto-style so that the rich flavours of the ingredients, stock and spices infuse the rice, whereas the Chinese typically like fried rice. So I'm making Portuguese-Chinese fried rice using a classic Portuguese sausage, chouriço, made from Iberian black pigs. Much like the Spanish chorizo, it is peppered with paprika and other flavoursome spices. When cooked, it leaches a delicious, reddish, spicy oil that gets absorbed by the starchy rice. Sweet baby scallops are my seafood of choice here. This dish will have your guests wanting more.

Serves 4 kcal 315 carbs 45.3g protein 13.3g fat 11.3g

Place the rice in a sieve and wash until the water runs clear to rinse away the excess starch. Place the rice in a medium pot, add 400ml water and bring to the boil. Once boiling, reduce the heat to low, cover the pan and simmer for 15-20 minutes until all the water has been absorbed and the rice is cooked through. Remove from the heat and fluff up the grains, then, to reduce the moisture of the rice, transfer to a tray and fan out - this will ensure the rice is dry enough to make the fried rice.

Heat a wok over a high heat until smoking, add the vegetable oil and give the oil a swirl. Add the garlic, shallots, chilli and spring onions and stir for a few seconds. Add the chouriço or chorizo pieces and cook for 30 seconds to crisp the edges, then add the baby scallops and toss together for 15 seconds. Season with the rice wine or dry sherry, then add the cooked rice to the wok and mix well so the rice absorbs all the flavours in the wok.

Season with the tamari or light soy sauce, salt and white pepper and toss well so that all the rice is turned a light brown. Add the lemon juice and toss the coriander through. Give it a final stir, then remove from the heat, transfer to serving bowls and serve immediately.

15 mins

2–3 mins

DIRTY HOISIN CRANBERRY KIMCHI PORK HOT CHEESE SANDWICH

100g pork loin, sliced thinly against the grain, on an angle
1 tablespoon Shaohsing rice wine or dry sherry
2 teaspoons rapeseed oil
1 red onion, sliced into rings
pinch of soft brown sugar

For the marinade
1 garlic clove, finely grated
1 teaspoon runny honey
1 teaspoon tamari or low-sodium light soy sauce
1 teaspoon cranberry jam
1 tablespoon hoisin sauce
½ teaspoon sriracha chilli sauce

Assemble with
2 slices of thick white bread
spread of mayonnaise
spread of Dijon mustard (optional)
50g medium Cheddar cheese, grated
small handful of baby spinach leaves
50g kimchi, roughly chopped
½ tablespoon finely chopped spring onion

My guilty pleasure since living in the UK is making naughty sandwiches. I love a hot sandwich and it's so comforting! This one is a mash-up of Chinese, Korean and British influences. The result is a fruity, spicy, fermented, porky savoury hot sandwich – it all sounds so wrong, but it's so right. Ideally, you'd make the cranberry jam yourself, as shop-bought can be on the sweet side, though you only need a bit of it. Serve with a fruity craft beer. Enjoy!

Serves 1 kcal 869 carbs 77.4g protein 50g fat 41.1g

Put all the ingredients for the marinade in a bowl and stir to combine. Add the pork slices, season with the rice wine or dry sherry and marinate for 10 minutes.

Heat a wok over a medium heat, add 1 tablespoon of the rapeseed oil and give it a swirl. Wok-fry the onion with the sugar until caramelised, then spoon out onto a plate.

Heat the wok over a medium-high heat, add the remaining rapeseed oil and give it a swirl. Add the marinated pork pieces and stir-fry for 2 minutes until cooked through. Set aside.

Spread one slice of bread with mayonnaise and the other with Dijon mustard, if you like. Top one slice with the cheese. Place the cheese-topped side under a preheated hot grill for 1–2 minutes to slightly melt the cheese. Remove from the oven and place the spinach on top of the cheese. Then add the slices of pork and the caramelised red onion and sprinkle with the kimchi and spring onion. Place the remaining bread slice on top, cut in half on the angle and serve immediately.

SPICY FOUR-PEPPER LAMB

350g boneless lamb loin, cut into
  square pieces
pinch of salt
pinch of ground white pepper
1 teaspoon cornflour
10 dried whole red chillies or
  small arbol chillies
1 teaspoon Sichuan peppercorns
2 tablespoons rapeseed oil
2 garlic cloves, chopped
2.5cm piece of fresh ginger,
  peeled and coarsely chopped
1 small jalapeño, deseeded and
  diced
1 green pepper, deseeded and
  sliced lengthways
1 star anise
2 tablespoons Chinkiang black
  rice vinegar or balsamic
  vinegar
1 tablespoon tamari or low-
  sodium light soy sauce
2–3 tablespoons chilli oil, or to
  taste

Here, delicious, chunky lamb is wok-fried with Sichuan
pepper, whole dried chillies, ginger, jalapeño, star anise and
green pepper. It's punchy and layered with heat, perfect for
the spice lover. This is not a one-wok process – you cook the
spices, the lamb and the pepper separately and then bring
them all together, a method that my grandmother would have
followed which ensures that every bit is wokked to perfection.
If you're feeling lazy, you can wok-fry the spices, add the lamb
and then add the pepper and seasoning – it will still be delish
and all will be forgiven. Perfect with jasmine rice.

Serves 4 kcal 312 carbs 7.1g protein 17.9g fat 24.4g

Put the lamb into a bowl, add the salt, white pepper and cornflour
and toss well to coat. Set aside for 5 minutes.

Heat a wok over a medium heat until smoking, add the dried
chillies and Sichuan peppercorns and toast, tossing continuously,
until fragrant and the chillies begin to blacken – about 10 seconds.
Transfer to a bowl and reserve.

Reheat the wok until smoking, then add 1 tablespoon of
rapeseed oil and give the oil a swirl. Add the lamb pieces to the
wok in an even layer and let it settle for about 1 minute until it
begins to brown. Then stir-fry the lamb vigorously for about 3
minutes until cooked through and medium-well done on the
inside. Transfer to a plate.

Reheat the wok over a medium heat, add the rapeseed oil and
give the oil a swirl. Add the garlic, ginger and jalapeño to the wok
and stir-fry for 1 minute until softened. Add the green pepper,
star anise and toasted chillies and peppercorns and toss until the
pepper is softened, about 2–3 minutes. Return the lamb to the
wok and cook until very hot. Add the vinegar and tamari or light
soy sauce and toss until well combined. Add the chilli oil and cook
until heated through. Transfer to a large, shallow serving plate and
serve immediately.

BEEF AND BLACK BEAN GREEN PEPPER NOODLES

For the beef

1 x 225g ribeye steak, excess
   fat trimmed off, cut into
   1.5cm-thick slices
1 teaspoon dark soy sauce
1 tablespoon cornflour
1 red bird's eye chilli, soaked in
   light soy sauce (to add a spicy
   edge to the dish), to garnish

For the rest of the stir-fry

2 tablespoons rapeseed oil
2 garlic cloves, finely chopped
2.5cm piece of fresh ginger,
   peeled and finely grated
1 red chilli, deseeded and finely
   chopped
1 teaspoon fermented salted
   black beans, rinsed and
   crushed (or shop-bought black
   bean sauce)
1 tablespoon Shaohsing rice wine
   or dry sherry
2 green peppers, deseeded and
   cut into julienne strips
1 tablespoon tamari or low-
   sodium light soy sauce
150ml hot vegetable stock
2 tablespoons cornflour, blended
   with 4 tablespoons cold water
400g cooked egg noodles
2 spring onions, sliced on the
   angle into 1cm pieces

This is based on the traditional Cantonese Beef with Black Bean Noodles. Dou-chi (fermented salted black beans) is a popular ingredient used across Southern China – from Sichuan in the south-west (where it is used in dishes such as twice-cooked pork) to Canton in the south-east (where it appears in dishes such as steamed seabass). It is made from soybeans that, once dried and salted, turn black during the fermentation process. The beans have an extremely salty flavour and are widely used in Chinese cookery – most famously to make black bean sauce. The ingredients that best complement this sauce are beef and green peppers. The green peppers have a fresh, raw, bitter-peppery bite that adds a savoury crunch, and cooked beef is deeply rich in umami, which enhances the salty black bean notes. This is a simple, quick stir-fry, the perfect midweek supper, which delivers on taste and is very easy to make. Tender beef fillet strips are sliced relatively thick, seasoned with some dark soy and wok-fried with aromatics, homemade black bean sauce and cooked egg noodles. You can add other vegetables too. Red chillies stir-fried with the dish, give a salty, spicy taste that is irresistible. If you are vegan, use chunky sliced smoked tofu instead of the beef and follow the rest of the recipe, or if you are not a fan of tofu, use a combination of fresh shimeji mushrooms and sliced shiitake mushrooms.

Serves 2   kcal 735   carbs 97.4g   protein 42.6g   fat 22.1g

Season the beef with the dark soy sauce and dust with the cornflour.

Heat a wok over a high heat until smoking, add the rapeseed oil and give it a swirl. Add the garlic, ginger and chilli and stir-fry for a few seconds to release their aroma. Add the black beans (or black bean sauce) and toss for 10 seconds, then add the beef and let it settle for about 10 seconds to brown the edges. Flip the beef over and when it starts to turn brown, add the rice wine or dry sherry to enrich the natural sweet flavour of the beef.

Add the green peppers and stir-fry for 1 minute, then season with the tamari or light soy sauce. Add the vegetable stock and bring to the boil, then stir in the blended cornflour to thicken the sauce. Stir in the cooked noodles and toss together well until all the ingredients are coated lightly in the sauce. Season further to taste, if you like. Divide between two plates, garnish with the soy-soaked bird's eye chilli and, for a fresh bite, the spring onions, and serve immediately.

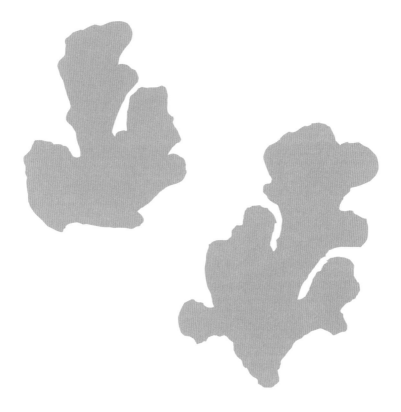

15 mins

8 mins

DF

PEANUT PORK SATAY RICE NOODLES

For the peanut sauce
30g toasted salted peanuts
1½ bird's eye chillies, roughly chopped
1 tablespoon fish sauce
1 tablespoon caster sugar
1 teaspoon sesame oil
1 teaspoon chopped coriander
juice of 2 limes

For the stir-fry
150g dried pad Thai rice noodles
1 tablespoon rapeseed oil
2.5cm piece of fresh ginger, peeled and sliced into coins
300g pork fillet, cut into 1cm-thick slices
1 tablespoon Shaohsing rice wine or dry sherry
1 tablespoon dark soy sauce
100g pak choy, leaves separated, stalks sliced into 2.5cm pieces
1 carrot, sliced on the angle
3 baby corn, sliced on the angle
150g mangetout
1 tablespoon tamari or low-sodium light soy sauce
30g roasted salted peanuts

For the garnishes
pinch of dried chilli flakes
1 lime, cut into 4 wedges
2 spring onions, sliced on the angle into thin slices

This is my stir-fry noodle version of a popular Thai street food snack. The best thing about this dish is that the sauce is so flavourful, all you have to do is choose your favourite crunchy vegetables and stir-fry it all together. I have chosen pak choy leaves and stalks, carrot, baby corn, mangetout and spring onions – a perfect 5-a-day vegetable fix. Simple and delicious for a mid-week supper. Wokky on!

Serves 2 kcal 793 carbs 83.5g protein 49.7g fat 28.9g

To make the peanut sauce, crush the peanuts in a pestle and mortar. Add the chillies, fish sauce, sugar, sesame oil and coriander and mash together until a thin paste forms. Add the lime juice and stir to mix well. Adjust the seasoning to taste if necessary. Set aside.

Soak the noodles in warm water for 10 minutes, then drain.

Heat a wok over a high heat until smoking, add the rapeseed oil and give it a swirl. Add the ginger and stir-fry for a few seconds to release its aroma and flavour into the oil. Add the pork slices and let them settle in the wok for a few seconds, then flip the meat over and toss until coloured and caramelised at the edges. As the pork starts to brown, add the rice wine or dry sherry and the dark soy sauce.

Quickly add all the vegetables and stir-fry for 1 minute. Add the peanut sauce and drained noodles, toss well and cook for another minute until all the ingredients are well coated in the sauce. Take off the heat and season with the tamari or light soy sauce. Sprinkle in the peanuts and give it one last toss.

To serve, divide the noodle mixture between two plates, add the chilli flakes, lime quarters and spring onion slices, to garnish.

SMOKY BACON SCALLOPS

200g large scallops, cleaned

pinch each of salt and white pepper

2 tablespoons rapeseed oil

5cm piece of fresh ginger, peeled and grated

100g smoked bacon lardons, diced

2 tablespoons Shaohsing rice wine or dry sherry

50ml hot vegetable stock

1 tablespoon tamari or low-sodium light soy sauce

1 tablespoon cornflour, blended with 2 tablespoons cold water

2 pinches of ground white pepper, to taste

1 tablespoon toasted sesame oil

1 spring onion, sliced thinly on the angle, to garnish

Scallops are a prized ingredient in Chinese cooking and symbolise wealth because of their resemblance to gold bullion. This is a great dish for a Chinese New Year party – the perfect sweetness of the scallops paired with the smoked salty bacon is brought together by your favourite Chinese condiments, giving a rich harmony of flavours.

Serves 2 kcal 406 carbs 11.2g protein 25.4g fat 28.2 g

Season the scallops with a pinch each of salt and white pepper.

Heat a wok over a high heat until smoking, add the rapeseed oil and give the oil a swirl. Add the ginger and stir-fry very quickly for a few seconds, then add the scallops and stir for a few seconds. Add the lardons and toss together for 1 minute, then add the rice wine or dry sherry. Pour in the hot vegetable stock and season with the tamari or light soy sauce.

Cook for 15 seconds, bringing the sauce to a bubble, then add the blended cornflour and stir all the ingredients well to coat them in the thicker sauce. Season further to taste with the white pepper and sprinkle on the sesame oil and spring onion.

Take off the heat, transfer to a serving dish and serve immediately with steamed vegetables and brown or jasmine rice.

5 mins

5 mins

GF DF

SPICY SMOKED BACON BROCCOLI

1 tablespoon rapeseed oil

2 garlic cloves, finely chopped

2.5cm piece of fresh ginger, peeled and finely grated

2 dried red chillies, torn

180g smoked bacon lardons, diced

2 tablespoons Shaohsing rice wine or dry sherry

1 large carrot, sliced in half lengthways, then in half again lengthways, then on the angle into 5mm-thick pieces

200g tenderstem broccoli, sliced on the angle into 2.5cm pieces

2 tablespoons Chinkiang black rice vinegar or balsamic vinegar

1 tablespoon tamari or low-sodium light soy sauce

Even a little bit of bacon goes a very long way. I'm a huge fan of smoked bacon lardons, they are full of flavour and when you pair them with some Chinese seasonings, crunchy carrots and tenderstem broccoli, the results are fabulous. Quick, simple and delicious every time.

Serves 2 kcal 360 carbs 13g protein 20.4g fat 25.5g

Heat a wok over a high heat until smoking, add the rapeseed oil and give it a swirl. Add the garlic, ginger and chilli pieces and toss for a few seconds. Quickly add the lardons and stir-fry for 1 minute until browned.

Add the rice wine or dry sherry, then add the carrot and broccoli and cook, tossing for 1 minute. Season with the vinegar and cook for 1 minute until the veggies are crisp, then add the light soy sauce. Toss together well and serve immediately with jasmine rice.

SICHUAN PORK AND FRENCH BEANS

1 tablespoon rapeseed oil

2.5cm piece of fresh ginger, peeled and grated

½ teaspoon toasted Sichuan peppercorns, left whole

1 red chilli, deseeded and finely chopped

150g minced pork

1 tablespoon Shaohsing rice wine or dry sherry

1 teaspoon dark soy sauce

200g French beans, sliced into 5mm rounds

1 teaspoon chilli bean paste

1 tablespoon lemon juice

1 tablespoon Chinkiang black rice vinegar or balsamic vinegar

1 tablespoon tamari or low-sodium light soy sauce

1 tablespoon chilli oil

1 teaspoon toasted sesame oil

large handful of coriander, finely chopped

This is a great way to cook French beans, but make sure they are fresh - when you buy them, snap them in half. If they make a crunchy snap, you know they are at their best and full of moisture and goodness. This dish may seem like a lot of ingredients, but most are seasonings from the store cupboard, just toss the beans in hot oil with ginger, Sichuan pepper, chillies and layers of seasoning and the dish is ready in minutes. This is a mini side dish that you would add as an accompaniment to rice and other dishes.

For vegans, substitute rehydrated soy mince for the minced pork, or you can use diced rehydrated dried Chinese mushrooms.

Serves 2 kcal 270 carbs 7.5g protein 23.4g fat 16.2g

Heat a wok over a high heat until smoking, add the rapeseed oil and give the oil a swirl. Add the ginger, Sichuan peppercorns and red chilli and toss for a few seconds. Add the minced pork and toss for 1 minute to crisp the edges of the pork. Season with the rice wine or dry sherry and add the dark soy sauce.

Add the French beans and toss well, then add a small splash of cold water to create some steam and stir-fry for 2–3 minutes until the beans are tender. Season with the chilli bean paste, lemon juice, vinegar, tamari or light soy sauce, chilli oil and toasted sesame oil.

Take off the heat, stir in the coriander and serve immediately with jasmine rice.

PORK, KIMCHI AND WATER CHESTNUT FRIED RICE

1 tablespoon rapeseed oil

2.5cm piece of fresh ginger, peeled and grated

200g minced pork

pinch of salt

1 tablespoon Shaohsing rice wine or dry sherry

225g can water chestnuts, drained and sliced

250g shop-bought kimchi, drained but reserve 1 tablespoon liquid

350g cooked jasmine rice

80g enoki mushrooms, cut into 1cm slices

2 tablespoons tamari or low-sodium light soy sauce

1 teaspoon clear rice vinegar or cider vinegar

1 teaspoon chilli oil

1 teaspoon toasted sesame oil

2 pinches of ground white pepper

2 spring onions, sliced on the angle, to garnish

I love my Asian fusion dishes, what I like to call Fusian – the combination of spicy pungent kimchi stir-fried with crunchy water chestnuts and tender sweet enoki mushrooms, makes for a delicious marriage in wok heaven. This unusual flavour combination is my invention and makes a simple but beautiful dish, perfect for entertaining.

If you're vegan, you can substitute rehydrated soy mince for the minced pork and just follow the rest of the recipe.

Serves 2 kcal 473 carbs 58.7g protein 29.9g fat 14.3g

Heat a wok over a high heat until smoking, add the rapeseed oil and give the oil a swirl. Add the ginger and toss for a few seconds, then add the minced pork and stir-fry for 1 minute until browned at the edges. Season with the salt and rice wine or dry sherry. Add the water chestnuts, kimchi and jasmine rice and stir-fry for 1 minute until the rice absorbs all the delicious flavours.

Add the enoki mushrooms, season with the tamari or light soy sauce, vinegar, chilli oil, sesame oil, white pepper and the reserved liquid from the kimchi. Toss gently together once more, then garnish with the spring onions and serve.

10 mins

70 mins

pre-cook, 40 mins braise-cook

GF DF

CHING'S BRAISED HONG SAO PORK

700g pork belly slices, rindless
2 tablespoons rapeseed or
    groundnut oil
1 tablespoon grated peeled fresh
    ginger
3 tablespoons Shaohsing rice
    wine or dry sherry
3 star anise
1 teaspoon whole Sichuan
    peppercorns
3 long whole dried red chillies
250ml chicken stock
80ml dark soy sauce
3 tablespoons soft brown sugar
pinch of salt

Another slightly longer dish. Regional variations on Hong Sao Rou, or red braised pork can be found across China. It is said to have been one of Chairman Mao's favourite dishes. Traditionally, belly pork pieces are cooked in a braising liquid of spices and sugar, the caramelised sugar imparting a rich brown colour. However, dark soy sauce is a popular way to enhance the umami salty-sweet flavour and I have used it in this dish. It adds depth and colour, giving the braising liquid a deep, reddy shine. The resulting pork should be sweet, salty and spiced and the sauce thick and sticky. I have reduced the amount of sugar to keep it healthier, but you can add more if you prefer a sweeter taste. It is best served simply with some steamed jasmine rice and stir-fried greens such as pak choy.

Serves 4 kcal 674 carbs 16.2g protein 49.1g fat 47g

Bring 1.5 litres water to the boil in a large pan. Add the pork belly slices and simmer over a medium heat for 30 minutes. Remove the pork and drain well, then pat dry with kitchen paper and slice into 2cm x 2cm pieces.

Heat a wok over a medium heat, add the rapeseed or groundnut oil and give the oil a swirl. Add the pork pieces and brown for 2 minutes, then add the ginger, rice wine or dry sherry, the star anise, Sichuan peppercorns, dried chillies, chicken stock, dark soy sauce, brown sugar and salt. Cover with a tight-fitting lid and cook over a medium heat for 45 minutes, until the liquid has reduced and thickened slightly and is a glossy reddish-brown colour.

Remove from the heat (see tip) and serve with steamed jasmine rice and stir-fried greens of your choice.

Ching's Tip
For a smooth cooked sauce, strain through a sieve and discard the whole spices, or you can just eat around them like the Chinese do!

20 mins

5 mins

DF

BLACK PEPPER BACON PINEAPPLE FRIED RICE

1 tablespoon rapeseed oil

2.5cm piece of fresh ginger, peeled and grated

150g smoked bacon lardons

1 teaspoon dark soy sauce

pinch of ground or cracked black pepper

6 large fresh shiitake mushrooms, sliced into 1cm strips

300g cooked jasmine rice

2 tablespoons tamari or low-sodium light soy sauce

100g fresh pineapple flesh, finely diced into cubes

1–2 spring onions, sliced on a deep diagonal, to garnish

To serve

sriracha chilli sauce

a few lime wedges (optional)

Who doesn't love ham and pineapple pizza? Hawaiian is one of my favourite pizza flavours and I can't get enough of it, so a bacon and pineapple fried rice is the next best thing. The black pepper helps to add a bit of heat and spice to complement the smoke of the bacon and the sweetness of the pineapple. For those who are sceptical about pineapple in fried rice, it's a staple dish and hails from the Yunnan region in China.

If you're vegan, you can lose the bacon and instead wok-fry some rehydrated cubed dried Chinese mushrooms, which are a great textured, earthy-smoky substitute.

Serves 2 kcal 466 carbs 49g protein 8.9g fat 22.8g

Heat a wok over a high heat until smoking, add the rapeseed oil and give it a swirl. Add the ginger and stir-fry for 5 seconds, then add the lardons and stir-fry for 1 minute to caramelise them around the edges. Season with the dark soy sauce and black pepper and toss well. Add the mushrooms and wok together for 30 seconds.

Tip in the cooked rice, season with the tamari or light soy sauce, then tip in the pineapple and stir gently to mix well. Garnish with the spring onions and serve with some sriracha chilli sauce. For an extra zing and a truly tropical taste, you can squeeze some lime juice over, if you like.

15 mins

8-9 mins

DF

PORKY CUMBERLAND SAUSAGE POT-STICKER DUMPLINGS

300g Cumberland sausages, skinned

50g tenderstem broccoli, stems only (reserve the heads for a wok-fry), blanched in boiling water for 10 seconds, drained and sliced into 5mm rounds

2 spring onions, finely sliced, to garnish

For the wrappers

1 packet wheat flour gyoza wrappers

1 tablespoon plain flour, plus extra for sprinkling

1 egg, beaten

1 tablespoon rapeseed or vegetable oil

For the dipping sauce

2 tablespoons HP Brown Sauce

2 tablespoons sweet chilli sauce

2 tablespoons tamari or low-sodium light soy sauce

Pot-stickers are so-named because they sometimes stick to the bottom of the wok. Adding a flour-water mix gives them crispy coating on the bottom. You can make a large batch, freeze them and cook straight from frozen. For a vegan version, substitute some finely chopped smoked tofu and some lightly mashed fresh tofu for the sausage in the filling.

Makes 10 kcal 141 carbs 11.6g protein 7.1g fat 7.4g

Lay out the wrappers on a wooden board sprinkled with a little plain flour. Spoon 2 teaspoons of the sausagemeat onto each and top with some broccoli. Seal the edges using a brush dipped into the beaten egg, then squeeze tight.

Heat a large, non-stick, shallow wok, add the rapeseed or vegetable oil and give the oil a swirl. Add the dumplings (making sure they don't touch each other) and cook for 30–45 seconds until the base is golden and crispy (they should lift up easily).

Meanwhile, working quickly, measure 250ml water into a jug, add the plain flour and whisk until most of the lumps are gone. Pour over the dumplings, cover and cook over a low-medium heat for 3–4 minutes until all the water has evaporated. Resist the temptation to remove the lid before the tops of the dumplings have a chance to cook through. Make sure the heat is not too hot, or the bottom of the dumplings will burn. However, if it is too low, the dumplings will go soggy and you risk some of them sticking. So, keep an eye on them – it helps to have a glass lid, so you can gauge if the floured water is on a gentle simmer.

Meanwhile, combine all the ingredients for the dipping sauce in a bowl and set aside.

Gently remove the dumplings from the wok (the flour water will have turned into a crispy and delicate flour sheet and should break easily when lifting the dumplings out of the wok). Arrange on a serving plate and drizzle with the dipping sauce, then garnish with the spring onions and serve immediately.

15 mins

5 mins

GF DF

CRISPY CHILLI BEEF QUICK CHEAT 'CONGEE'

300g sirloin steak, fat removed, finely sliced into matchstick strips
2 tablespoons cornflour
600ml sunflower oil

For the sauce
2 tablespoons tamari or low-sodium light soy sauce
2 tablespoons sweet chilli sauce
juice of 1 small orange

For the quick cheat congee
300g cooked jasmine rice
550ml hot vegetable stock
1 tablespoon tamari or low-sodium light soy sauce
1 teaspoon toasted sesame oil
pinch of ground white pepper

To serve
1 carrot, cut into julienne strips
2 spring onions, finely sliced lengthways
chilli oil (optional)

This combines two of my favourite comfort foods into one dish – comforting 'congee' (although a quick cheat version) and crispy chilli beef. The result is one helluva moreish dish!

If you're vegan, you can use fried strips of tofu or sliced fresh shiitake mushrooms.

Serves 2 kcal 583 carbs 72.2g protein 41.8g fat 16.3g

Put all the ingredients for the congee in a medium pan, add 100ml boiling water, mix well and bring to a simmer, then keep over a low-medium heat.

For the crispy beef, dip the beef strips in the cornflour and shake off any excess. Place on a plate. Heat a wok over a high heat and fill to a third of its depth with the sunflower oil. Heat the oil to 180°C or until a cube of bread turns golden brown in 15 seconds and floats to the surface. Deep-fry the beef until golden, then drain on kitchen paper.

While the beef is draining, make the sauce. Heat a small wok, add the tamari or light soy sauce, sweet chilli sauce and orange juice and cook until thickened. Add the beef strips and toss until they are all coated in the sauce.

To serve, divide the congee between two bowls, dress each with some julienned carrot, then top with crispy chilli beef and sprinkle on the spring onions. If you like, spoon some chilli oil around the edges, then serve immediately.

MISO HONEY RIBS

600g pork ribs, chopped into
    3–4cm lengths
sunflower oil, for shallow-frying
1 spring onion, sliced on the angle
    into thin slices, to garnish

For the marinade
pinch of salt
pinch of ground white pepper
1 tablespoon red miso paste
1 tablespoon tamari or low-
    sodium light soy sauce
1 tablespoon mirin

For the sauce
2 garlic cloves, finely chopped
2 tablespoons mirin
1 tablespoon red miso paste
2 tablespoons tamari or low-
    sodium light soy sauce
1 tablespoon soft brown sugar
1 tablespoon runny honey

This is perfect party finger food. Marinating the ribs in red miso paste for 20 minutes means the flavours get absorbed before you wok-fry them.

If you're vegan, you can make large chunky tofu dippers and then follow the rest of the recipe, frying the tofu until golden, and substitute the honey for golden syrup.

Serves 4 kcal 415 carbs 15.7g protein 29.2g fat 26.1g

Put all the ingredients for the marinade into a large bowl and stir to combine. Add the pork ribs and turn to coat, then cover the bowl and leave to marinate for at least 20 minutes, or for as long as possible, in the fridge.

Meanwhile, combine all the ingredients for the sauce in a bowl and set aside.

Heat a wok over a high heat until smoking, then fill to a quarter of its depth with sunflower oil. Heat the oil to 180°C or until a cube of bread dropped in turns golden brown in 15 seconds and floats to the surface. Using a spider, carefully lower half the ribs into the oil and shallow-fry until cooked through and browned.

Lift the ribs out of the wok with the spider and drain on kitchen paper. Repeat with the other half. Drain the wok of oil through a heatproof colander into a heatproof bowl and wipe it clean, then reheat over a high heat.

Add the sauce to the wok and cook over a low-medium heat for 5–6 minutes until the sauce has reduced to a sticky consistency. Toss the ribs back in and stir to coat. Garnish with the spring onion and serve immediately.

GF DF

FIVE-SPICE PORK WITH BABY PAK CHOY

2 tablespoons rapeseed oil

2 pinches of salt

2 garlic cloves, crushed

2.5cm piece of fresh ginger, peeled and finely chopped

1 teaspoon Chinese five-spice powder

250g sliced pork loin

1 tablespoon Shaohsing rice wine or dry sherry

1 tablespoon tamari or low-sodium light soy sauce

1 teaspoon dark soy sauce

200g baby pak choy, leaves separated

50ml hot vegetable stock

1 teaspoon cornflour, blended with 1 tablespoon cold water

This is a straightforward, home-style Chinese dish. It can be varied in lots of ways, but I love the simplicity of Chinese five-spice, ginger, rice wine and soy – these are the flavours I call comfort and 'home'.

To make this one vegan, lose the pork and substitute with meaty oyster mushrooms.

Serves 2 kcal 411 carbs 7.5g protein 35.6g fat 26.6g

Heat a wok over a high heat until smoking, add the rapeseed oil and give it a swirl. Add the salt, garlic, ginger and five-spice powder and cook for a few seconds. Add the pork slices and let them settle in the wok for a few seconds, then flip the meat over and toss until coloured and caramelised at the edges.

As the pork starts to brown, add the rice wine or dry sherry and cook until evaporated. Season with the light and dark soy sauces. Add the pak choy and toss together for 1 minute until the leaves have wilted. Add the hot vegetable stock, bring to a bubble, then stir in the blended cornflour and cook briefly. Give it a final toss and take the wok off the heat. Transfer to serving plates and serve immediately.

5 mins

33 mins

DF

PORK, GINGER AND DUCK EGG CONGEE

1 quantity Classic Plain Congee 'Zhou' (see page 52)

2 'thousand-year-old' duck eggs, sliced into eighths

1 tablespoon rapeseed oil

2.5cm piece of fresh ginger, peeled and finely sliced

200g pork fillet, finely sliced

1 tablespoon Shaohsing rice wine, dry sherry or vegetable stock

3 fresh shiitake mushrooms, rinsed and finely diced

2 tablespoons tamari or low-sodium light soy sauce

pinch of salt

pinch of ground white pepper

dash of sesame oil (optional)

2 spring onions, sliced on the angle

fried dough bread sticks, shop-bought, sliced into 5mm rounds, to serve (optional)

This is a variation on the classic congee recipe on page 52, and one of my favourite breakfasts. The famous cha chaan teng shops in Hong Kong (especially the ones located in the old wet market at Canton Road in Kowloon) sell similar steaming bowls of pork, ginger and duck egg congee. My aunt would go shopping early for ingredients in the wet market and then reward herself with a steaming bowl of this congee – it's so comforting.

Serves 4 kcal 342 carbs 43.7g protein 21g fat 10.5g

Make the congee as directed on page 52, then 5 minutes before the full cooking time, add the duck egg pieces.

Heat a separate wok over a high heat until smoking, add the rapeseed oil and give the oil a swirl. Add the ginger and stir quickly, then add the pork slices and stir quickly. Add the rice wine, dry sherry or vegetable stock and the diced mushrooms. Season with the tamari or light soy sauce.

Add the ginger pork stir-fry to the congee and stir in well. Season the congee with the salt and white pepper. Add a dash of sesame oil, if you like, and sprinkle on the sliced spring onions. Serve with bread stick slices, if you have some. Yum!

10 mins

5 mins

GF DF

SICHUAN BACON
AND LEEK WOK-FRY

1 tablespoon rapeseed oil

1 garlic clove, crushed

1 teaspoon whole Sichuan
peppercorns

150g smoked bacon lardons

1 tablespoon Shaohsing rice wine
or dry sherry

2 baby leeks, cut at a 45° angle
into 5mm slices

1 tablespoon tamari or low-
sodium light soy sauce

1 tablespoon Chinkiang black
rice vinegar or balsamic
vinegar

1 teaspoon chilli oil

½ teaspoon toasted sesame oil

Mmm... bacon and leek. Such a great combo, particularly in this smoky, Sichuan-inspired stir fry. It's my cheat go-to when I want the flavours of the classic Sichuan twice-cooked pork, but a quicker, speedier fix. Perfect with jasmine rice.

If you're vegan, use smoked tofu chunks instead of the smoked bacon lardons.

Serves 2 kcal 283 carbs 4.1g protein 13.4g fat 23.7g

Heat a wok over a high heat until smoking, add the rapeseed oil and give the oil a swirl. Add the garlic and Sichuan peppercorns and toss for a few seconds. Add the lardons and stir-fry for 3 minutes until caramelised at the edges, then add the rice wine or dry sherry. Add the leeks and toss for 1 minute, adding a small dash of water around the edge of the wok to help create some steam. Once the leeks are wilted, season with the tamari or light soy sauce, vinegar, chilli oil and sesame oil. Serve immediately with plain jasmine rice.

5 mins

3 mins

DF

SOY MISO BEEF WITH SICHUAN PICKLE AND COURGETTES

1 x 400g ribeye steak, cut into
    2cm chunky slices
1 teaspoon cornflour

For the marinade
1 tablespoon red miso paste
1 tablespoon soft brown sugar
1 tablespoon tamari or low-
    sodium light soy sauce
1 teaspoon dark soy sauce
1 garlic clove, finely chopped
2.5cm piece of fresh ginger,
    peeled and finely grated

For the stir-fry
2 tablespoons rapeseed oil
100g baby courgettes, cut on a
    deep angle into 1cm slices
1 tablespoon Shaohsing rice wine
    or dry sherry
80g Sichuan pickled mustard in
    chilli oil, drained and cut into
    strips

For the garnish
1 red cayenne chilli, finely sliced
    into rings (deseed, if you like)
1 teaspoon toasted sesame
    seeds

This is a juicy ribeye steak stir-fry with tons of flavour in which I fuse two ingredients – rich Japanese red miso and pungent Sichuan pickled mustard in chilli oil. Both are strong flavours, but there's no clash here – it's a great Asian fusion wok fry! The chilli adds a super delicious heat and spice and the miso brings the deep savoury notes. Delicious and perfect served with jasmine rice.

If you're vegan, substitute large meaty Portobello mushrooms for the steak.

Serves 2 kcal 494 carbs 18.3g protein 46.7g fat 26.2g

Place the beef in a shallow container. To make the marinade, pour 50ml cold water into a jug. Add the miso paste and stir well to dissolve. Stir in the sugar and light and dark soy sauces. Add the garlic and ginger and stir well to combine, using a whisk. Pour this marinade over the beef and leave for 5 minutes.

Heat a wok over a high heat until smoking, add the rapeseed oil and give the oil a swirl. Dust the marinated beef with cornflour and place together with the marinade into the wok and sear on one side for 30 seconds. Flip it over. For rare steak, cook for 30 seconds, for medium, toss for a minute, or for well-done, cook for 1 minute.

Add the courgettes and cook for another 30 seconds, then season with the rice wine or dry sherry and cook until evaporated. Add the pickled mustard and toss well to combine.

Garnish with the chilli rings and sesame seeds and serve with jasmine rice.

15 mins

3-4 mins

DF

OYSTER SAUCE BEEF AND BROCCOLI

1 tablespoon rapeseed oil

3 garlic cloves, finely chopped

2.5cm piece of fresh ginger, peeled and grated

1 red cayenne chilli, sliced

1 sirloin steak approx. 250g, excess fat trimmed off, cut into 1cm slices

1 tablespoon Shaohsing rice wine or dry sherry

250g tenderstem broccoli, sliced on the angle into 2.5cm pieces

1 tablespoon dark soy sauce

large handful of beansprouts

2 tablespoons tamari or low-sodium light soy sauce

2 tablespoons oyster sauce

Oyster sauce and beef are the perfect partners for each other! Oyster sauce is so rich and savoury it brings out the naturally occurring glutamates in the beef, which gives it that more-ish savoury quality. And beef and broccoli are also great together – the meaty soft goodness of the beef marries well with the crunchy sweet florets and stems of the broccoli. A match made in heaven and made complete when served with jasmine rice or noodles.

If you are vegan, substitute chunky cubes of fried tofu and a handful of fresh shiitake mushrooms for the beef. You can also substitute mushroom sauce (available in Chinese supermarkets or online) for the oyster sauce.

Serves 2 kcal 274 carbs 12.5g protein 31.9g fat 11.1g

Heat a wok over a high heat until smoking, add the rapeseed oil and give the oil a swirl. Quickly add the garlic, ginger and chilli and stir-fry a few seconds. Add the beef and stir-fry for a few seconds.

As the beef starts to brown, add the rice wine or dry sherry and follow quickly with the broccoli. Stir-fry together for 30 seconds, then add the dark soy sauce and toss well.

Add the beansprouts and toss together, then season with the tamari or light soy sauce and oyster sauce. Stir-fry for less than 1 minute, then serve immediately.

5 mins

3-4 mins

GF DF

DOFU RU LAMB WITH GAI LAN

For the broccoli stir-fry
1 tablespoon rapeseed oil
pinch of salt
1cm piece of fresh ginger, peeled and sliced into matchsticks
1 small bird's eye red chilli, sliced
350g gai lan (Chinese broccoli) or broccolini
1 tablespoon Shaohsing rice wine or dry sherry

For the lamb stir fry
1 tablespoon rapeseed oil
2 small garlic cloves, roughly chopped
200g lamb neck fillet, cut on the angle into 1cm slices

For the sauce
1 tablespoon Shaohsing rice wine or dry sherry
5g dofu ru (fermented soybean curd)
1 tablespoon tamari or low-sodium light soy sauce
50ml cold vegetable stock
1 teaspoon cornflour
pinch of soft brown sugar
pinch of cracked black pepper

This is an easy home-wokked lamb dish. Delicious and simple. Serve with wok-fried Chinese broccoli (included here too) and jasmine rice.

Serves 2 kcal 347 carbs 10.6g protein 29.3g fat 21.2g

Mix all the ingredients for the sauce in a jug and stir well, using a whisk.

For the broccoli stir fry, heat a wok over a high heat until smoking, add the rapeseed oil and give the oil a swirl. Add the salt, then the ginger and chilli and stir-fry for a few seconds. Add the gai lan or broccolini and stir-fry for 1 minute. Season with the rice wine or dry sherry and stir-fry for another 2 minutes. Spoon out onto warm serving plates.

For the lamb stir fry, reheat the wok until smoking, add the oil and give the oil a swirl. Add the garlic and toss for a few seconds, then add the lamb. Leave to settle for a few seconds, then stir-fry until almost cooked. Add the sauce, bring to a bubble and cook until the sauce has reduced to a sticky consistency. Spoon out on top of the gai lan and serve immediately.

30 mins

10 mins

DF

PORK AND CHINESE 'SHUI-JIAO' – 'WATER-COOKED' DUMPLINGS

200g Chinese leaf stalks, finely diced
60g carrots, finely diced
10g salt
1 garlic clove, grated
30g fresh ginger, peeled and finely grated
300g lean minced pork mince
1 vegetable stock cube, grated
10g caster sugar
pinch of white pepper
dash of Shaohsing rice wine or dry sherry
dash of toasted sesame oil
30g spring onions, finely diced
12 shop-bought fresh square wheat flour dumpling wrappers
1 spring onion, sliced into strips and soaked in iced water for 5 minutes to curl, drained, to garnish

For the dipping sauce
3 tablespoons toasted sesame oil
3 tablespoons tamari or low-sodium light soy sauce
3 tablespoons clear rice vinegar or cider vinegar
1 teaspoon sriracha chilli sauce
1 red chilli, deseeded and finely chopped
few sprigs of coriander, roughly chopped

*per dumpling

Dumplings symbolise prosperity so are perfect to welcome in the Chinese New Year. If there are any left at the end of the meal (which I doubt!), they can be refreshed in boiling water, or fried in a lightly oiled, non-stick pan for a crispy coating. Enjoy!

Makes 12 kcal 98 carbs 8.7g protein 6.8g fat 4.1g*

Place the Chinese leaf stalks and carrots in a bowl. Rub the salt into the vegetables, cover the bowl and leave in the fridge for about 30 minutes. After 30 minutes, squeeze dry the vegetables using your hands and discard the water.

Combine all the ingredients for the dipping sauce in a bowl and set aside.

Add the garlic, ginger and minced pork to the vegetables, season with the stock cube, sugar, white pepper, rice wine or dry sherry, sesame oil and diced spring onion and mix well using your hands. Throw the mixture in the bowl a few times to aerate the filling, then gather into a large ball – it should come together like a dough and not be overly sticky.

Spoon 1½ teaspoons of the mixture into the centre of a dumpling wrapper. Dip your finger into a small bowl of water and run it along the edges of the wrapper. Fold and pleat the edges, pinching them well until the edges are firmly sealed. Repeat with the remaining filling and wrappers.

Once all the dumplings have been folded and sealed, drop them into a wok of boiling water. Return to the boil, then turn the heat down to a simmer and cook the dumplings for 3–4 minutes. The dumplings are cooked when they all float to the surface.

Remove the dumplings with a large slotted spoon, drain well and place on a serving plate. Garnish with sliced fresh spring onion curls and serve with the spicy dipping sauce.

Glossary

Bamboo shoots
These add a crunchy texture to dishes. Boiled bamboo sprouts are also pickled in brine, giving them a sour taste, and in chilli oil, which gives them a spicy taste.

Chilli bean paste
Made from broad beans and chillies that have been fermented with salt to give a deep brown-red sauce. Some versions include fermented soybeans or garlic. Good in soups and braised dishes, it should be used with caution, as some varieties are extremely hot.

Chilli oil
A fiery, orange-red oil made by heating dried red chillies in oil. To make your own, heat groundnut oil in a wok, add dried chilli flakes with seeds and cook for 2 minutes. Take off the heat and leave the chilli to infuse in the oil until completely cooled. Decant into a glass jar and store for a month before using. For a clear oil, pass through a sieve.

Chilli sauce/chilli garlic sauce
A bright red, hot sauce made from chillies, vinegar, sugar and salt. Some varieties are flavoured with garlic and vinegar.

Chinese celery
Chinese celery stalks are slimmer and more tender than the Western variety and the flavour is more intense. Both the stalks and leaves are used.

Chinese leaf/cabbage
This has a delicate, sweet aroma with a mild flavour that disappears when cooked. The white stalk has a crunchy texture and remains succulent even after prolonged cooking. The Koreans mainly use it for kimchi.

Chinese chives (garlic chives)
Long, flat, green leaves with a strong garlic flavour. There are two varieties, one has small yellow flowers at the top, which can be eaten. Both are delicious.

Chinese five-spice powder
A blend of five spices – cinnamon, cloves, Sichuan peppercorns, fennel and star anise – that give the distinctive sour, bitter, pungent, sweet and salty flavours of Chinese cooking. This spice works extremely well with meats and in marinades.

Chinese sesame paste
Made from crushed roasted white sesame seeds blended with toasted sesame oil, it is used with other sauces to flavour dishes. If you cannot find it, you can use tahini instead, but it is a lot lighter in flavour so you will need to add more toasted sesame oil.

Chinese wood ear mushrooms
Dark brown-black fungi with ear-shaped caps. Very crunchy in texture, they do not impart flavour but add colour and crispness. They should be soaked in hot water for 20 minutes before cooking – they will double in size.

Chinkiang black rice vinegar
A strong aromatic vinegar made from fermented rice. The taste is mellow and earthy and it gives dishes a wonderful smoky flavour. Balsamic vinegar makes a good substitute.

Choi sum
A green leafy vegetable with a thick stem and tender leaves that belongs to the Brassica family, it is delicious either steamed or stir-fried. Tenderstem broccoli is a good substitute.

Cinnamon stick/bark
The dried bark of various trees in the Cinnamomum family. It can be used in pieces or ground. Ground adds a sweet woody fragrance.

Congee
Plain soupy rice porridge that can be combined with other ingredients, such as salted peanuts, fermented bean curd, and chilli-pickled bamboo shoots.

Daikon (white radish)
Resembling a large white carrot, this crunchy vegetable has a peppery taste and pungent smell, and is eaten raw, pickled or cooked. It contains vitamin C and diastase, which aids digestion. Koreans use it to make kimchi.

Dofu/fresh bean curd – Described as the 'cheese' of China, this is made from soybean curd and is quite bland, but takes on the flavour of whatever ingredients it is cooked with. Called tofu in Japan and dofu in Chinese, dofu, it is high in protein and also contains B vitamins, isoflavones and calcium. Available as firm, soft and silken, the firm variety is great in soups, salads and stir-fries. Silken has a cream cheese-like texture. *Dofu gan* is dried firm smoked beancurd.

Dried Chinese mushrooms
These need to be soaked in hot water for 20 minutes before cooking. They have a strong aroma and a slightly salty taste and therefore complement savoury dishes well.

Egg noodles
Made from egg yolk, wheat flour and salt, and available fresh or dried, these come in a variety of thickness and shapes – flat and thin, long and rounded like spaghetti, and flat and coiled in a ball.

Enoki mushrooms
Tiny, white, very thin, long-stemmed mushrooms with a delicate flavour. Used raw, they add texture to salads. Lightly steamed, they are slightly chewy.

Fermented salted black beans
Small black soybeans preserved in salt, which must be rinsed in cold water before use. They are used to make black bean sauce.

Fermented yellow bean paste
Made from yellow soybeans, water and salt. A cheat substitute would be hoisin sauce, though this is sweeter and not as salty.

Fish sauce
A light amber liquid extracted from fermented fish and salt. The first press – made without additives or sugar – is the most prized.

Gai lan (Chinese broccoli)
Unlike Western green broccoli, gai lan comes in several varieties, some with yellow flowers, though most have large, glossy blue-green leaves with long, thick and crisp chunky stems. A good substitute is Tenderstem broccoli.

Goji berry (Chinese wolfberry)
The deep red, dried fruit of an evergreen shrub. Similar to a raisin, it is sweet and nutritionally rich.

Hoisin sauce
Made from fermented soybeans, sugar, vinegar, star anise, sesame oil and red rice, this is great used as a marinade and as a dipping sauce.

Jasmine rice
A long-grain white rice originating from Thailand that has a nutty jasmine-scented aroma. You need to rinse it before cooking until the water runs clear to get rid of any excess starch.

Kaffir lime leaves
The leaves of the citrus fruit native to tropical Asia. The leaves emit an intense citrus aroma.

Kimchi
A Korean staple made from salted and fermented Chinese cabbage mixed with Korean radish, Korean dried chilli flakes, spring onions, ginger and *geotgal* (salted seafood).

Lemongrass (citronella root)
A tough, lemon-scented stalk popular in Thai and Vietnamese cuisines. Look for lemon-green stalks that are tightly formed, firm and heavy with no bruising, tapering to a deeper green towards the end.

Mock duck
A vegetarian ingredient made from wheat gluten, soya, sugar, salt and oil. A good substitute is bean curd or tofu skin.

Mirin
A sweet Japanese rice wine similar to sake, with a lower alcohol content but a higher sugar one (the sugar occurs naturally as a result of the fermentation process).

Miso paste
A thick Japanese paste made from fermented rice, barley, soybeans, salt and a fungus called *kojikin*. Sweet, earthy, fruity and salty, it comes in many varieties depending on the types of grains used.

Mung bean noodles
Made from the starch of green mung beans and water, these noodles come in various thicknesses, vermicelli being the thinnest. To use, soak in hot water for 5–6 minutes before cooking. If using in soups or deep-frying, no pre-soaking is necessary. They become translucent when cooked.

Mushroom oyster sauce – see oyster sauce

Nori (dried seaweed)
Sold in thin sheets, this is usually roasted over a flame until it turns black or purple-green. Used as a garnish or to wrap sushi, once opened, a pack must be sealed and stored in an airtight container or it loses its crispness. If this happens, just roast the sheets over an open flame for a few seconds until crisp.

Oyster mushrooms
Soft and chewy with a slight oyster taste, this white, yellow or grey oyster shaped fungi is moist and fragrant.

Oyster sauce
A seasoning sauce made from oyster extract that can also be used as a marinade. A vegetarian variety is also available. It is very salty, so taste the dish before adding.

Pad Thai noodles
Flat noodles, 5mm wide, made from rice. They need to be soaked in hot water for 5 minutes before cooking.

Pak choy
A vegetable with broad green leaves, which taper to white stalks. Crisp and crunchy, it can be boiled, steamed or stir-fried.

Panko breadcrumbs
Made from bread without crusts, these Japanese breadcrumbs have a crisp texture.

Potato flour
A smooth, gluten-free flour made from potatoes that are steamed, dried and then ground. It gives wonderful crispness when used to coat ingredients before frying.

Red miso paste – see Miso paste

Rice vinegar
A clear (white), mild vinegar made from fermented rice. Cider vinegar can be used as a substitute. Chinese black rice vinegar is a rich, aromatic vinegar that is used in braised dishes and sauces, and with noodles. When cooked, it gives a smoky flavour with a mellow and earthy taste. Balsamic vinegar makes a good substitute.

Sake
A fermented Japanese drink made from polished rice that is brewed in a similar way to wine. Its alcohol content ranges from 15–20%.

Sesame seeds
These oil-rich seeds add a nutty taste and a delicate texture to many Asian dishes. Available in black, white/yellow and red varieties, toasted and untoasted.

Shaohsing rice wine
Made from rice, millet and yeast that has been aged for 3–5 years, it takes the 'odour' or 'rawness' out of meats and fish and gives a bittersweet finish. Dry sherry makes a good substitute.

Shiitake mushrooms
These large, nutrient-rich, dark brown umbrella-shaped fungi are prized for their culinary and medicinal properties. The dried variety needs to be soaked in water for 20 minutes before cooking.

Shimeji (beech) mushrooms
These come in white or brown varieties, and are characterised by long stems and tight concave caps.

Shrimp paste
A dry, smooth paste made by adding salt to shrimp or fish broth, this is then stored overnight, drained and sun dried. The mixture is then ground and left to ferment in an earthenware jar. A good paste should be dark deep purple.

Sichuan peppercorns
Known as 'Hua jiao' in Mandarin or 'flower pepper', these have a pungent, citrusy aroma. They can be wok-roasted, cooked in oil to flavour the oil, or mixed with salt as a condiment.

Soy sauce
Made from wheat and fermented soybeans, soy sauce is available in dark and light varieties. Dark soy sauce is aged a lot longer than the light variety, and is mellower and less salty. Light soy sauce is used in China instead of salt. Wheat-free varieties, called tamari, are available, though it is quite salty. You can also buy low-sodium varieties.

Sriracha chilli sauce
A hot sauce made from chilli peppers, distilled vinegar, garlic, salt and sugar. It is named after the coastal town of Si Racha, Eastern Thailand.

Star anise
The fruit of a small evergreen plant, these are called *bajio* or 'eight horns' in Chinese. They have a distinct aniseed flavour and are one of the ingredients found in Chinese five-spice powder.

Tamari – see Soy sauce

Toasted sesame oil
Made from white pressed and toasted sesame seeds, this oil is used as a flavouring/seasoning and is not suitable for use as a cooking oil since it burns easily. The flavour is intense, so use sparingly.

Tofu – see Fresh bean curd

Vermicelli mung bean noodles – see Mung bean noodles
Vermicelli rice noodle
Similar to vermicelli mung bean noodles, they come in many different widths and varieties. Before cooking, soak in hot water for 5 minutes. If using in salads, soak for 20 minutes. If using in a soup, add them dry.

Water chestnuts
The roots of an aquatic plant that grows in freshwater ponds, marshes and lakes, and in slow-moving rivers and streams. Unpeeled, they resemble a chestnut in shape and colouring. They have a firm, crunchy texture.

Wheat flour noodles
Thin, white dried noodles. Do not confuse these with thick Japanese udon noodles.

Yellow bean sauce
Made from fermented yellow soybeans, dark brown sugar and rice wine, this is a very popular flavouring ingredient in Sichuan and Hunan province in China. It also makes a great marinade for meats. Yellow bean paste is a thicker consistency and is used in marinades and as a flavouring in many savoury dishes.

Zha cai (Sichuan vegetable)
A popular Sichuan pickled mustard vegetable used in hot and sour soups and dan dan noodles. The knobbly fist-sized stems are salted, pressed, dried and then covered in hot chilli paste and fermented in an earthenware jar (similar to that of Korean kimchi). The taste is spicy, salty and sour with a crunchy texture. Excess salt can be removed by soaking in fresh water. Usually sold in vacuum packs either whole or ready sliced.

Index

Acknowledgments

I owe a big thank you to my publisher Joanna Copestick, my editorial director Judith Hannam, and Heather Holden Brown my literary agent and Kate Heather, my agent at RH Talent – without these four incredible women, *Wok On* would not have been born! Thank you so much for your belief and for your support for what I do. I am so lucky to have you all.

I must thank the incredibly talented and hardworking team I was so blessed to have! Thank you to editorial assistant Isabel Gonzalez-Prendergast and my copy editor Barbara Dixon for your attention to detail. Thank you to Caroline Clark for the fabulous cover design of the book and the funky illustrations. More than a few vintage bottles of champagne go to the incredible Tamin Jones for the photography, the hugely talented Aya Nishimura for the beautiful food styling, and of course the one and only Wei Tang for the props, as well as special thanks to Gemma John for the production of the book. This book really is a testament to your talents and would not have been made so beautiful without each and every one of you.

Biggest thanks and love to Chef Tom Kerridge for his amazing quote and support, as always. An idol and huge culinary hero of mine, I am indebted, and it means so much to have your support.

Thank you to Michael Kagan at ICM Talent and assistant Colin Burke in the US for continuing to support my career and for believing in me.

Thanks to all the powers at BBC, ITV, Food Network UK and US, Cooking Channel, NBC for continuing to give me opportunities and allowing me to share my cooking on the telly.

To all my family near or far, especially my mum and dad, thank you for all the sacrifices you made in order to give us a better life. I wouldn't be here without you and I am so proud of how far we have all come. This book is also for my three grandmas – Wu, Huang and Longhurst – thank you for your inspiration.

To Jamie, my husband, the vegan recipes I concocted for you are now in ink! Thank you for wokking with me through all that life throws at us, I can't imagine another wokker I would rather share my life with!

A huge thanks to all my fans – past and present – for continuing to support me on this culinary journey, this book is for you. I hope you are happy with the book and enjoy the recipes as much as I have in creating them. I am indebted and ever grateful for your love.

Writing a book isn't easy but I enjoy the process immensely and really this book is for all the cooks at home who have supported me time and again, over the years, it's you that I write the recipes for and I hope they give you as much joy as they do me, and that they sustain you and your family as your support has sustained me over these years.

I am truly grateful for this crazy journey...this girl that once grew up on a farm in southern Taiwan and ended up cooking on the telly in the UK, your support has made my dreams come true and not a day goes by that I don't pinch myself.

Thank you from my heart, for your love and kindness, this girl will continue to Wok On... and hopefully do you proud.